ALLEN COUNTY PUBLIC LIBRARY

FORT WAYNE, INDIANA 46802

You may return this book to any agency, branch, or bookmobile of the Allen County Public Library.

GROWTH
WITH
FAIRNESS

A PROGRAM TO REBUILD AMERICA'S ECONOMY

MILTON J. ESMAN
STEVEN I. JACKSON
RONALD F. KING

Seven Locks Press
Cabin John, MD / Washington, DC

Copyright © 1988 by Milton J. Esman, Steven I. Jackson, and
Ronald F. King

Library of Congress Cataloging-in-Publication Data

Esman, Milton J. (Milton Jacob), 1918-
  Growth with fairness.

  Bibliography: p.

    1. United States—Economic policy—1981-
I. Jackson, Steven I. II. King, Ronald Frederick,
1949-   . III. Title.
HC106.8.E85   1988   338.973   88-4682
ISBN 0-932020-56-9
ISBN 0-932020-57-7 (pbk.)

Design by Giles Bayley
Cover by Betsy Bayley
Typesetting by Bets LTD

Printing by Sheridan Press

Manufactured in the United States of America.

First edition, May 1988

SEVEN LOCKS PRESS
P.O. Box 27
Cabin John, MD 20818
(301) 320-2130

*Seven Locks books are distributed to the trade by the
National Book Network, Lanham, MD.*

Contents

Contents

PREFACE

The authors of this book are members of the Department of Government at Cornell University. Milt Esman's specific field of expertise is comparative politics and public administration, Steve Jackson's is international political economy, and Ron King's is domestic public finance. In the past, our individual publications have been addressed primarily to academic and professional readers. What has impelled us, then, to collaborate on this venture and direct it to a much wider audience of concerned citizens?

The idea for *Growth with Fairness* originated from a series of conversations, starting quite informally but gaining definition over time, held in Milt's office during spring of 1987. It was clear to us that the Reagan era, rapidly drawing toward its close, had inflicted terrible damage on the American economy and on the fabric of American society. It seemed equally clear that unless the damage were corrected during the next few years, we could anticipate the long-term decline of the U.S. position in world markets, the reduction in our living standards, and the fading of the American dream. We became convinced that these negative trends could and must be reversed and the U.S. economy restored to its traditional path of dynamic, competitive growth combined with expanded opportunities for all. The turnaround, however, would require bold and decisive policy measures.

We debated the policy prescriptions currently in fashion among moderates and liberals. Some we found useful, but many were insufficient to the critical tasks at hand. Those proposals we thought plausible were being offered as individual ideas, apart from any integrated conceptual framework essential for a systematic attack on the nation's ills. The time has long passed for ad hoc reforms and piecemeal correctives. We therefore sought to outline a compelling vision for a progressive future, consistent with the best in the American historical tradition and capable of mobilizing public support and motivating policymakers. Within this framework, we designed a series of policy initiatives—politically and financially feasible—which, when enacted into law, could move our economy in the required direction. These initiatives, as presented here, are grouped into four sections: industrial policy, trade policy, human resources policy, and budgetary policy. Together they form a package intended to reinvigorate U.S. competitiveness and growth while distributing the resultant benefits fairly among our fellow citizens.

We allowed this project to develop from casual conversations to a "white paper" circulated among friends and then to a book manuscript principally because we are concerned that the Democratic party is being much too cautious with new ideas. It is not enough to be against Reaganomics; it is necessary to be for a reasonable alternative. As we approach the critical presidential election of 1988, the Democratic party must expose the paltry and uneven gains generated by the so-called Reagan recovery and the tenuous foundations upon which it rests. It must draw attention to the looming burden of debt, the precipitous decline of our industrial base, the dangers of the present U.S. position in the world economy, and the shameful increase in poverty at home. It must offer the American voter more than a warmed-over version of Reaganomics with a more human face. The American people have historically turned to the Democratic party in times of trouble, but only because it has offered constructive and pragmatic solutions. The Democrats must reverse the negative image of government that has been propagated by the Republicans. In the future as in the past, our representative government, under a Democratic president, can serve as the instrument of our collective will. Its policies and programs can make a positive contribution—indeed they are essential—to restoring our society to the path of sustained, competitive growth combined with fairness.

As professors, we direct our research efforts to analyzing the strengths and weaknesses of modern democratic government, the changing social and economic context within which it operates, and the means to make it function better. As authors of this manuscript, we offer a positive, practical, and responsible set of policy proposals that point the way to the economic future the American people desire and deserve. Every four years, under our Constitutional system, the American citizenry is asked to evaluate the candidates for the nation's highest office and the policies they propose. The policies outlined below comprise the core of a program we believe should be adopted and advocated by the Democratic party as it faces the historic challenge of 1988 and beyond.

This manuscript was completed just prior to the collapse of the stock market on October 19, 1987 and the dramatic decline in the value of the U.S. dollar that followed in its wake. Several readers of the white paper that preceded this manuscript admonished us that our analysis might not be taken seriously because of the widespread view that, despite some unresolved problems, the U.S. economy was in good shape. The stock market was booming, unemployment was down, and the recovery was continuing. This illusion has since been shattered, yet two months after the crash we see little evidence that our political leadership is facing up to the political realities that confront our country. Some still seem to hope that this crisis will miraculously go away; others hope that symbolic patchwork with the federal budget will somehow restore confidence. The American people, however, sense that our economic problems have deeper roots that are not amenable to quick fixes. They expect candor, not evasion from their political leadership, and especially from the Democratic party. We are convinced that the economic bad news of the past several weeks confirms the underlying correctness of our analysis and that bold policies such as those we recommend are needed to restore growth and fairness to our troubled American economy.

In preparing this book, we especially would like to thank our publisher, James McGrath Morris, who convinced us to put away our various scholarly monographs in progress and instead to devote the past few months to this most enjoyable project; our editor, Maia Ambegaokar, for her efforts in turning the work of three independent-minded scribblers into a unified and even readable manuscript; and our research assistant, Kasia Grzelkowski, who often discovered in the library what we could not find ourselves. We also gratefully acknowledge the helpful contributions from numerous colleagues and friends who advised us on facts and sharpened our arguments. In particular, we would like to mention Robert C. Browne, Jerome Ziegler, Robert R. Nathan, Judith Reppy, Milton Leitenberg, Ned Lebow, the Honorable Matthew F. McHugh, William F. Whyte, Kenneth Robinson, Dan Wirls, Marcia Whicker, Andrew Dunham, and Paul Peretz. Ron King thanks the Jonathan Meigs Fund for its support. This book is dedicated to Janice, Maia, and Rona, for their understanding.

Ithaca, New York
December 1987

GROWTH

WITH

FAIRNESS

A PROGRAM TO REBUILD AMERICA'S ECONOMY

Chapter 1:

REDEEMING THE AMERICAN TRADITION

Americans are a people of plenty. Our country was settled largely by men and women driven by the pursuit of economic abundance and individual liberty. That pursuit is written into our culture and our national institutions. It affects our judgment of individual achievements and political leaders. We are also an enterprising people, and we have enjoyed unprecedented success as economic innovators, producers, and consumers. We are abundantly blessed with the natural resources, human skills, and technological capabilities needed to fulfill our material needs and aspirations. We have provided the motivation for individuals to better themselves through their productive efforts. We have protected opportunity and rewarded initiative. And as we have come to regard sustained economic growth as the key to improved living standards for all, America has become the leading nation in an integrated world economy that fosters peace, cooperation, and growth around the globe.

In recent years, however, we have faltered. The U.S. economy has been stagnating for the past 15 years. Real median family income has remained stationary. Inequality and poverty have increased. Our productivity, the key to growth and competitiveness, has lagged behind that of our main industrial rivals. Millions of jobs have been lost in manufacturing and farming, and hundreds of stable communities have been devastated. Much of U.S. business is no longer competitive, either abroad or at home. Massive and persistent trade deficits demonstrate the painful truth that much of our industry has lost its technological edge. Massive and persistent budget deficits demonstrate that the federal government has lost the ability to generate resources sufficient to meet its needs. The United States now consumes more than it produces, and we finance the gap by heavy borrowing, much of it from overseas. These are not the characteristics of a strong and healthy economy.

The Reagan administration's economic policies further weakened this nation at a time when the American people expected renewed strength. After the deepest recession since the Great Depression, these policies created the appearance of an economic recovery, but that recovery was deceptive, dangerous, and discriminatory. It was deceptive because it left major sectors of the economy behind. It was dangerous because future expansion cannot be achieved without addressing the underlying cause of America's loss of competitiveness in domestic and international markets. It was discriminatory because it extended benefits primarily to the richest American families and cost the middle class and the poor both income and security. Faced with an already troubled U.S. economy, the administration, with its free market platitudes, failed at growth and abandoned fairness.

Guided by a commitment to growth, fairness, and responsible government, the American people now demand and expect fundamental changes from Reagan's misguided policies, policies which have undermined the foundations of our nation's future prosperity. We also now recognize that Reaganomics has in act subverted the central values of our society. Before the failures of the Reagan era become irreversible, we must reinvigorate our economy and repair the damages to our society. Drawing on the joint efforts of our public and private institutions, and inspired by the main traditions of our national experience, we must directly confront these serious challenges. The program for Growth with Fairness presented here charts a return to a positive course of expanding opportunity. It relies on America's historic faith in the common sense of its people and in their ability to act vigorously and pragmatically. Only with such a program can we build a secure future for ourselves, our children, and our grandchildren.

The Economic Legacy of the Reagan Era

Despite a lingering affection for President Reagan as a person, large numbers of Americans have begun to look upon the ideology, priorities, and performance of his administration as a brief but harmful aberration in the historical development of American democracy. The reactionary French monarch, Louis XIV, whose profligacy bankrupted the French treasury and left his successors to cope with mountainous debts and the disastrous consequences of foreign misadventures, proclaimed shortly before his death, "After me, the deluge." Like him, Reagan leaves a legacy to his successors that will include the unenviable task of cleaning up and repairing the damage. His fiscal irresponsibility, ideological dogmatism, and mean-spirited policies have imposed serious costs upon the American economy and society.

The Reagan administration inherited an economy that was already in trouble, suffering the combined effects of recession and inflation, the loss of international competitiveness, and the transfer of domestic manufacturing operations abroad. On the demand side, the Johnson administration's delay in obtaining a tax increase to finance the unpopular war in Vietnam precipitated the inflationary pressures that persisted throughout the 1970s. Consumer costs escalated, wage-price agreements disintegrated, and future expectations became unsettled. On the supply side, two oil shocks revealed to Americans the scarcity of basic resources and our vulnerability to international economic fluctuations. At the same time, multinational corporations, which had previously invested abroad primarily to gain access to foreign markets, began on a large scale to transfer production to Third World countries merely to take advantage of low wages. At home, this period witnessed the ascendancy of financial and legal experts as top corporate managers, who introduced in their wake an excessive concern with money manipulation and short-term profit taking. By contrast, our major trade competitors, especially Japanese and German enterprises, were investing heavily in the modernization of their products and production processes and were expanding their shares of world markets. No economy, not even one as strong and resilient as ours, could long escape the combined effects of detrimental underinvestment, sluggish productivity, and rising consumer expectations.

As a result, the U.S. economy has been essentially stagnant for a decade and a half. In real terms, average family income has remained unchanged while family debt has more than doubled. More than two-fifths of all families with children have seen their real incomes decline by more than 15 percent, while the real average income of all families with children has fallen by more than 6 percent. The apparent economic gains of the past few years have been due primarily to the extraordinary rise in financial speculation and to the creation of low-wage, insecure service-sector jobs, which fail to provide for the hopes and dreams of a large number of Americans. More than 40 percent of all jobs in the United States in 1986 paid $11,000 or less per year. More than 17 million working Americans have no health insurance to cover their medical needs. The number of poor people has grown dramatically. Virtually 20 percent of our children live in poverty despite government welfare assistance, an appalling prospect for any society.

Meanwhile, growth in U.S. productivity, the precondition

for sound economic expansion and rising living standards, has fallen behind that of other industrial nations, and so have net savings and investment. We have lost our competitive edge. U.S. industry is no longer number one, no longer able to compete in foreign markets or even at home. Our massive trade deficit is now running at an annual level of $160 billion, or 4 percent of the gross national product (GNP). Many of our industries—including steel, automobiles, textiles, machine tools, and electronics—have consistently lost market shares. The workers, managers, and communities that depend on them increasingly face disaster. Even our proudest industries, those in high technology and agriculture, are in deep trouble; we now import more high-tech and food products than we sell abroad.

Instead of improving an unsatisfactory situation, the Reagan administration's misguided policies dealt crippling blows to the future of the American economy. The centerpiece of the administration's solution to these problems was the 1981 tax bill, which slashed federal income tax rates and greatly increased business depreciation allowances. The main beneficiaries were corporations and wealthy individuals in the top income brackets, on the implausible assumption that leaving more disposable income in their hands was the only policy step needed to revitalize American industry. All blame for our economic condition was laid on the public sector, which the administration believed was artificially restraining natural expansionary forces. The Reagan remedy was simply to cut back on the nonmilitary activities of government.

This misconceived fiscal strategy became a dangerous one because it slashed federal taxes regardless of federal expenditures. Reagan substantially reduced receipts while increasing military outlays enormously, and the result has been budget deficits that have averaged more than $200 billion a year between 1983 and 1987. The U.S. Treasury has been forced into heavy borrowing, more than doubling our national debt since the self-styled "conservative" Reagan presidency began. Borrowing has strained our very limited domestic savings and forced the United States to turn to foreign capital, making us dependent upon others to maintain our solvency. The burden of the interest charges paid by the American taxpayer is now $136 billion per year, comprising nearly 14 percent of the federal budget, and this proportion is rising steadily.

Borrowing to finance the federal debt helped push U.S. interest rates astronomically high, causing U.S. firms to pay high prices for their investment funds, much higher than the cost of raising capital in Germany or Japan. As a result, our industry has been compelled to defer needed capital projects, delaying the modernization of manufacturing operations and further impairing its ability to compete.

Moreover, the need to maintain an inflow of funds to support the Reagan deficits raised the exchange value of the dollar relative to other currencies. This put U.S. firms, even the most efficient among them, at a great disadvantage when exporting abroad while it opened our markets to a flood of underpriced foreign goods. Some American plants were driven out of business, and some firms accelerated the transfer of production overseas. Increasingly the label "MADE IN THE USA," once the proud emblem of quality goods, has come to mean the U.S.-based assembly of parts and components manufactured abroad by sweatshop labor under a practice euphemistically termed *outsourcing*. Americans now import much more than we export, and we consume much more than we produce. The consequence during the first five years of the Reagan administration was a net loss to U.S. workers and their communities of more than one million reasonably well-paid manufacturing jobs, while internationally our move from a creditor nation to the world's largest debtor has further strained an already fragile world monetary system.

Borrowing can be a good thing if done in moderation and if the money is used to build for future strength. Our present debt, however, is being accumulated not to finance economic expansion, but rather for current consumption by government and families. To preserve living standards, our households have resorted to borrowing of their own; household debt has reached the staggering level of more than $300 billion, having multiplied by two-and-one-half times since 1981. All told, this profligate borrowing has doubled as a share of GNP. It is an unseemly tax on future generations. It is a source of political vulnerability to the whims and pressures of foreign banks, corporations, and governments. Our society, until recently a production machine that was the envy of the world and the source of the highest material living standards ever achieved, is now consistently living beyond its means.

The Reagan administration, however, was sublimely indifferent to these trends, which its ill-conceived policies helped to create. Its trickle-down tax policies, which anticipated that high-income taxpayers would invest their tax savings in job-producing industries, failed dismally. Instead, the wealthy have channeled their higher after-tax incomes into speculative paper and luxury consumption. The growth that our economy has registered in the last few years has not been in the production of commodities, nor even primarily of useful services, as the apologists for the present administration claim. Rather, paper gains have been registered primarily in real estate, financial operations, corporate takeovers, and related unproductive activities, which serve as breeding grounds for immoral and, as we see increasingly, illegal insider profiteering.

The United States is now in the fifth year of the so-called Reagan economic recovery. Yet increases in the GNP have exceeded population growth only slightly. Unemployment, which soared to double-digit numbers during the 1982–83 Reagan recession, has finally come down to Carter administration levels. The escalating number of discouraged workers, those who want to work but have given up the active search for employment, has swollen the real number of unemployed Americans to more than 13 million people. Inflation, which had slowed because of the collapse of oil prices and the wage restraints imposed on U.S. workers, is showing signs of moving back up again. The Reagan recession was so deep that family income declined in real terms (adjusting for inflation) from its 1979 levels by more than 10 percent. The subsequent recovery has been so shallow that even in 1986 real family incomes had not returned to the levels of the Carter years. Under Reagan, households in the upper 20 percent have seen their incomes rise by nearly one-tenth; households in the lower 20 percent have seen their incomes fall by almost that amount. Real wages for factory workers actually have declined. Almost half of all new jobs created between 1979 and 1985 pay $7,400 or less per year. A large proportion of those new jobs are in dead-end occupations, offering little hope of advancement. Cutbacks in federal programs have particularly hurt the working poor. Even with the rise in two-earner families, it has become increasingly difficult for the average family to own a home or purchase the other amenities normally associated with a middle-class American standard of living.

Americans must hear the echoes of Herbert Hoover, who, in the depths of the Great Depression of the 1930s, similarly reassured our unemployed workers and bankrupt farmers that prosperity was just around the corner. Hunger and homelessness in cities and on farms have failed to disturb the comforting Republican ideology that smaller government and marketplace magic will someday solve all our economic and social problems. In contrast to Reagan's empty assurances, Americans see an economy that is malfunctioning and out of control, that has imposed the main burdens of adjustment on average working people and low-income citizens while the wealthy enjoy unprecedented affluence.

We must not fool ourselves, however, into thinking that quick fixes will solve our problems. Quick fixes—balanced budget amendments, protectionist tariffs walls, exorbitant interest rates on consumer credit—will bring misery, not relief, in the long run. We can stop living beyond our means at the budgetary, trade, and consumer levels by forcibly reducing our standards of living; but that is a prescription for social frustration and painful sacrifice, and it is unnecessary. On the other hand, we can stop living beyond our means by increasing the means, and that is the prescription for sustained growth, genuine prosperity, and social harmony.

While advocates of the quick fix see basic problems in the

U.S. economy but offer no solution capable of restoring sound economic growth, President Reagan blithely promised growth but failed to recognize the symptoms of an unhealthy economy. Confronted by accumulating evidence of decay, of the collapse of our goods-producing sectors, and of an impending crisis in financial markets, the Reagan administration clung to its faith in the "miracle of the market." It refused to admit responsibility for debilitating fiscal and trade deficits and refused even to consider the requisite corrective actions, except belatedly to reduce the exchange rate value of the dollar. Instead, the administration assumed that all distortions would automatically disappear if the government simply kept its hands off.

It should be no surprise to objective observers that higher interest rates have not succeeded in stimulating greater domestic savings, that lower tax rates have not succeeded in stimulating greater productive investment, and that the recent sharp fall in the international exchange value of the dollar has not succeeded in stimulating greater trade competitiveness. Our industries cannot be destroyed one day and miraculously summoned back to life the next. The sad truth is that many of them have been hurt badly. Too much of their machinery is now obsolete and their product designs outdated. Too many skilled engineers, managers, and workers have been discharged. Too many multinationals have lost interest in manufacturing in the United States. Market adjustments are helpful in a free enterprise economy, but it is intellectual dogmatism to assert that those adjustments are all that is needed. Having contributed by its mismanagement to our current economic impasse, the Reagan administration must also be condemned for offering no practical or constructive strategy for dealing with it.

This is not a time for false hopes and illusions. The only sure road that leads away from stagnation is that of higher productivity and competitiveness. The budget deficit can be brought down, the trade deficit reduced, and consumer credit restrained only by a vigorous and sustained program to rebuild America's industrial capacity. More production with more jobs at decent wages will generate added tax revenues while reducing social welfare expenditures. More production of goods that are competitive in quality and price will allow us to pay our import bill without borrowing. More workers earning livable incomes will limit the need to survive on borrowed money.

The program outlined in this book is designed to assist in rebuilding the American economy and to ensure that the benefits of this renewed growth are shared fairly among our citizens. It does not promise quick fixes, and it does not rest on blind faith in marketplace miracles. Instead, this program directly confronts the enormous task before us.

We must restore our commitment to our high economic ideals, but not by dogmatically rejecting the use of public policies that promote real growth. We must increase our productive capacity, but in a way that fully uses the skills and talents of our work force. We must increase our international competitiveness, but not by turning America into a low-wage country. We must bring the federal budget deficit under control, but not by further decimating those government services essential for future growth with fairness. In sum, we must direct our national efforts—public and private, state and federal—to restoring the kind of prosperous economy that America and its citizens deserve. These are urgent national tasks if America is to avoid further deterioration of our industry and resume our place among the leading countries in the world economy.

To Build for the American Future

America will emerge from the dead ends and shambles of the Reagan years and will resume its national march toward a society about which we can be proud. Throughout our history, retrenchment and reaction have regularly been followed by expansion and progress. McKinley was succeeded by Theodore Roosevelt; Taft was succeeded by Wilson; Harding, Coolidge, and Hoover were succeeded by Franklin Roosevelt and Truman; Eisenhower was succeeded by Kennedy and

Johnson. The Reagan wave has exhausted itself. The time has come to plan for the future.

We must analyze in depth what went wrong with the Reagan policies, why they did not engender sound economic growth, and how they affected deleteriously the lives of so many people. We must then design policies that will better serve the national interest. Our discussions will be improved to the extent that economists and other social scientists contribute their technical expertise. Yet the outcome of our deliberations should not be merely a technical exercise. It should incorporate as far as possible the preferences and practical reasoning of our democratic citizenry. It should be based on principles that Americans have affirmed for two centuries and that we consider essential to the constitution of our society and to our optimistic image of the future.

There are four themes to which we Americans have returned time and time again in our efforts to root pragmatic solutions to contemporary problems in a vision of America's destiny:

- the need for a responsible and supportive government;
- the importance of a dynamic, productive, and competitive private economy;
- a commitment to social fairness for all Americans; and
- a patriotic pride that is positive and unifying in outlook.

These themes motivate and inspire this program for Growth with Fairness and are reflected in the specific policy recommendations presented in this book. They are intrinsic to the American tradition. Nevertheless, they seem to have been forgotten or repudiated since 1981.

A Responsible and Supportive Government

From the beginnings of our Republic, our founding fathers looked upon the federal government as an institution necessary to "promote the general welfare," as mandated by the preamble to the Constitution. Our government was designed to be a responsive institution, attentive to the dreams and demands of individuals, families, and communities. On the one hand, the founders recognized the lesson of history— that government power can abuse the rights of free citizens; thus, they established internal checks and balances that have for the most part succeeded in protecting our liberties, as in the recent cases of Watergate and Irangate. On the other hand, they also recognized that there are abuses against the public and individual citizens that require the application of government power; thus, they delegated to the central political authority the capacity to oversee national economic conditions and to ensure that the economy expanded from sound foundations. This tension—between limited government and useful government—runs throughout American history. Each era has sought its own point of compromise, fashioned pragmatically so as to advance our mutual needs and interests.

In our national experience, a vigorous role for government has been recognized as critical to prosperity. From the protective tariffs for our infant industries during Washington's presidency, to the plans for internal improvements under Jackson, to the homestead land distribution under Lincoln, to the transcontinental railroad, to the regulation of monopolies, to the management of the macroeconomy, the public sector has played a partial but essential role in the development of American productivity. Its specific policies and overall leadership have contributed, in different ways in different eras, to the promise of opportunity and the affluence that has made our country a leader among industrial nations.

Demagogic attacks on government have obscured the fact that the public sector is an agent of our democratic will, that it regularly speaks for us and on our behalf. It is our collective arm, the means by which we as a people act together in the effort to construct a better society. Surely government cannot and ought not attempt everything. The burden of proof should always fall on those who would add to or expand public activities. A fair and productive nation, however, must look to government not as an enemy, but as an instrument available to us to deal with our common problems and meet our common needs. We look to government as the servant of our public interest, as shaped and refined by the machinery of our representative institutions.

Americans believe in government that is responsible as well as responsive. A responsible government should assess carefully the consequences of its policies, their general effect on society as a whole, and their specific effects on the lives of the diverse individuals who together form the social fabric of America. That government should be above the temptation to pursue short-term political advantages at the expense of future generations. It should not promise more than it can deliver. Responsible government should keep its own financial and administrative affairs in order, for disorder in government can create havoc in our economy. Government, however, also has a more positive role to play. The public sector is unique in its obligation to guide and assist other institutions of society. From its location at the center of things, it should help us to define and achieve our aspirations.

America's tradition of supportive and responsible government rests on cooperation not only between the public and private spheres, but also between the different levels of government. *Federalism* is the term applied to relationships between the states and the central government. In America, unlike in many other countries, power and responsibility are apportioned intricately among federal, state, and local authorities. According to the Constitution, some powers are assigned to Washington while others are reserved for the states. Institutions at each level maintain their autonomy, yet they must also cooperate to achieve practical results. They must apportion the tasks of government pragmatically, not by being insular but by recognizing appropriate differences. They must work in partnership to consolidate a nation out of 50 parts rather than to "devolve" into separate and segmented spheres. The object is to secure both national standards and local responsiveness, to provide some overall direction for policy while allowing its adaptation to particular conditions. The specific proposals advanced herein involve the judicious use of government, at both the federal and the state level, to help improve the quality of life for all our people.

A Prosperous, Productive, and Competitive Private Economy
The American people have always shared a pride in our national capacity for economic growth. From the earliest days of our Republic, we have been committed to unleashing the tremendous potential inherent in a free people and to building the foundations for sustained and sustainable prosperity. On the farms and in the textile mills of the late 1700s, we produced from the land and its products those goods that satisfied our material needs. With the railroads and the steel mills of the late 1800s, we moved with confidence into the ranks of the world's industrial powers. From automobile plants and refrigerator factories in the twentieth century, the best consumer durables emerged. Dynamic growth in productive capacity changed us rapidly from a nation of small farmers and tradesmen to the world's most prolific producer of wealth.

Since the turn of the century, one of our great sources of national pride lay in the assurance that, through the most innovative methods, America was among the world's leaders in the efficient production of useful, high-quality goods. That is what "Yankee know-how" is all about. Goods made by U.S. workers in U.S.-owned and -managed firms dominated our large and expanding domestic market. Although we were less strongly export-minded than some, we competed effectively in international markets. In high technology, we were preeminent. Our fertile farmland became the breadbasket for much of the world. Based on this comparative advantage in manufactured and agricultural production, from 1894 until the 1970s we enjoyed a favorable balance of trade with the rest of the world.

Our enterprising American character has generated efficient production and a standard of living that is the envy of the world. We have always been able to earn enough in international competition to finance the essential imports that we require and that contribute to our choices as consumers. Further, we and our families and communities have prospered as a consequence of the livable wages resulting from productive jobs. With sustained growth, we have maintained and reaffirmed throughout our history a commitment to honest labor, opportunity, and upward mobility that has served as our distinguishing cultural mark and the foundation of the American dream.

Manufacturing useful goods at competitive prices in the world economy has made us a prosperous nation. However, in recent years, we have lost sight of the critical importance of maintaining our productive capabilities. Because of an unhealthy emphasis on the short-term bottom line, our industrial managers have neglected the longer-run efforts needed to build a sound foundation for the future. All too often, they have wasted both their energies and their capital in purely unproductive and parasitical activities, in corporate raiding and in merger mania. We have become a country of money manipulators. Speculation now dominates production. Exchange now dominates efficiency. Therefore, top priority for our economic development during the next two decades must be assigned to the competitive expansion of our goods-producing industries—to their design, engineering, and manufacture; to their quality, price, and reliability; to their marketing and servicing—so that U.S. goods can once again hold their own in world and domestic markets.

Fortunately, the work ethic is very much alive in our society. Some of our management practices have lagged, some of our engineering and craft skills may have grown rusty, and some of our plants and equipment are outdated, but our essential resource base—our raw materials, talents, and ambitions—remains intact. It is waiting to be motivated by appropriate government leadership, nurtured by effective government policies, and stimulated by feasible government incentives. However, we will not be able to rebuild a sound economy by making money from money. Our economic future depends on making *things* again, for they are what will give value to our money and meaning to our work. We must reject the false belief that market drift will automatically engender sufficient and secure GNP growth. We must instead chart a policy intended to revive and enhance the capacity, creativity, and competitiveness of the productive sectors of our economy. Thus, reinvigorating our manufacturing industries is the central challenge faced by an effective strategy for America's economic renewal.

A Commitment to Social Fairness for All Americans

Born in a rebellion against unfair treatment, America's first two centuries have been filled with struggles to extend to all Americans our national commitment to fairness. This concept has become increasingly inclusive. The inalienable rights that the Declaration of Independence attributed to all men have been gradually extended to women as well. Our nation, which at its founding accepted the bondage of slavery for Blacks, has gradually extended the equal protection of the laws to members of all races and ethnic minorities. Children have been protected from the oppression of hard labor and assured extensive free public education. Gradually, our industrial workers won protections on the job and guarantees that they would have some security in their retirement. Throughout this century, we have recognized increasingly the importance of broadening and deepening our sense of fairness.

The American tradition of democratic citizenship holds that all able-bodied adults should assume responsibility for supporting themselves and their dependents. In that same tradition, Americans believe that those who falter on the way, through ill-fortune or their own inadequacies, should be helped to become self-sufficient as quickly as possible for the sake of their own self-respect and in the interest of society. Americans also believe that those who are unable to earn a livelihood because of chronic incapacity or disability should be maintained at levels consistent with human dignity by government, assisted where possible by voluntary and community agencies. The role of government in caring for the disabled and helping the victims of adverse circumstances is merely the extension to a modern, urbanized nation of the practices of neighborly assistance, generosity, and charity that have characterized our society since its first settlements. In his 1984 keynote address to the Democratic National Convention, Governor Mario Cuomo of New York reminded us that Americans have historically thought of our nation as a large family, which attempts to care for its members when they experience hard times and which helps them in practical ways to return to self-reliance and self-support. As individuals and as a society, we are morally impoverished when we forsake that ideal.

The American vision is one in which all citizens, not merely a favored few, can look forward to a life that, culturally and materially, represents an improvement over the conditions that were available to their parents. Over our history, this expectation by and large has been fulfilled, but it can no longer be taken for granted. Most young Americans can no longer realistically look forward, as their parents could, to ever owning their own home, to planning for a comfortable retirement, or to building a career that promises advancement. In the past, during times of relative stagnation, we have had faith in the progress that comes from restored economic growth. Again, today, the restoration of economic vitality will help lift the incomes of many working Americans. Yet we have always known, as well, that GNP growth will not alone be sufficient. Improvements at the aggregate level must be translated into specific improvements at the level of real individuals. Public policy can help ensure that America's renewed growth is generated and distributed in a manner that is fair to our citizenry. A rising tide cannot be considered a social good if it lifts only the easily buoyant but leaves large numbers of us behind to drown.

Americans have never believed that social fairness is an obstacle to economic success. Indeed, it is a necessary condition for the kind of success that is consistent with our national ideals. We have never accepted the view that economic growth for the nation as a whole demands that some of our citizens must suffer. This has never been the American way. We have recognized that our national productivity largely depends on the skills and the diligence of our work force, and that our national affluence is defined in large measure by the purchasing power available to the ordinary wage earner. The American dream has always been inclusive. This is the hope that has brought generations of immigrants to our shores. This is the confidence that has given generations of our workers the drive to achieve.

During the 1980s, America has stopped making progress in the area of social justice. In celebrating the motivation of selfish interest, the Reaganites forgot that the sum of self-interest does not always equal the general interest. In celebrating the dynamics of marketplace competition, they forgot that the losers also deserve consideration. We are not a mere collection of autonomous economic atoms, but a people committed to mutual support and development. Within the limits of our resources and guided by the spirit of individual freedom, public policy can help provide the skills, ensure the opportunity, protect the rights, and guarantee the security necessary for an inclusive prosperity. The time has come to return to the best in our American tradition. We need to restore America to the paths of sustained economic growth and compassionate social fairness, and we need to integrate the two paths, so that the nation as a whole and all the individuals within it can advance toward the future together.

A Patriotic Pride That Is Positive and Unifying in Outlook
Love of country and pride in its institutions and achievements are signs of a healthy society that includes all its citizens within a network of mutual concern, opportunity, and responsibility. Such a society preserves an honored place for all its members, rewarding excellence and extending care and compassion to those who falter. A truly patriotic society draws on all its resources—public and private, local and national—to strengthen the family, protect the natural heritage, promote the material and cultural quality of life, build supportive communities, and respect the endowments

of our diverse citizenry in a pluralistic society.

A patriotic society will vigilantly defend its borders and meet its international commitments. It does not, however, require saber-rattling militarism, nor bullying rhetoric, nor jingoism, nor empty boasting about our superiority. True patriotism is not expressed in aggressive and unlawful adventurism in the Middle East or Central America, nor in the cynical distortion of treaty obligations, nor in the flouting of findings by international tribunals. It is not reflected in shifting all blame for our lack of international competitiveness onto others, nor in selfish trade policies that impose severe costs on the world economy. Rather, true patriotism is based on a quiet appreciation of the beauty of our land, the honor of our traditions, and the aspiration to continually better ourselves and our communities. Ultimately, our strength depends far more on the productivity and resilience of our economy and on the health and spirit of our families and communities than on the amount of sophisticated weaponry we accumulate. Patriotism consists of deep concern with the direction America is pursuing and of serious debate about the alternatives before us, not of the mindless echoes of bombastic slogans. It is reflected primarily in the internal qualities of our society, not on the quantity of fear we induce in foreign relations.

Patriotism commits us to build upon the best features of our society, and it inspires us with a vision of the future. That vision has always emphasized that America is a society of people rather than classes. Madison in the Federalist Papers warned against the dangers of unchecked factions. DeTocqueville, writing in the mid-1800s, noted that our nation's most distinctive characteristic was a spirit of individual equality, without the entrenched or inherited hierarchies of aristocratic Europe. Our dedication has been to a society based on talent, in which all individuals are guaranteed the opportunity to achieve their potential. Once a revolutionary creed, it has been a source of admiration and emulation by nations around the world.

We must guard against those tendencies that can sharply

divide us by race and by economic class. We must reject public policies that make us more unequal, more stratified, and less compassionate. We must remain concerned with the opportunities available to every American. Paradoxically, our commitment to individualism is itself the source of our solidarity. We are best united when we stand together on behalf of the separate interests of each of us, when we give full recognition to the talents inherent in every person, when we work to help each individual thrive through his or her own special contribution to our national development.

Americans expect their leaders to articulate the ideals that unite us, that give us cohesion despite our differences, and that advance our sense of collective national purpose. Our commitment to the vision of a flourishing individual in a flourishing society has been and remains the core of our patriotism. As Lincoln remarked in 1854,

> The legitimate object of government is to do
> for a community of people whatever they need
> to have done, but cannot do at all, or cannot so
> well do, for themselves, in their separate and in-
> dividual capacities.

Program for Growth with Fairness

The specific proposals for Growth with Fairness presented here do not address the totality of our individual needs and national aims. They focus mainly on economic realities and refer to the spiritual, cultural, social, and political dimensions of our lives only in passing. A healthy and just economy, however, provides the essential material base for the realization of our other individual and collective goals. For that reason, it receives special attention here. Equally, not all economic matters lie within the limited influence of government in a free enterprise society. Government policy is emphasized here because it is through the policy process that we deliberately articulate our national goals and undertake conscious steps to achieve them. Economic policy certainly does not encompass all that is meaningful to the American people. It is, however, indispensable to the construction of the kind of society most Americans seek.

Our government, in the past, has been reluctant to use its influence over the private economy. We have on occasion opened the fiscal taps, but we have barely regulated the flow. As long as our economy was clearly dominant in the world, we were satisfied merely to know that, as long as our corporations had ample capital and our consumers had ample demand, productive markets would take care of themselves. We can no longer operate with such optimistic expectations. The time has come for government—federal, state, and local—to use more of its legitimate leverage to help direct our economic energies into socially productive channels.

Decisive leadership will be required from the private sector as well as from government over the next decade. Above all, the United States must begin to reinvest on a large scale, to modernize and expand our lagging manufacturing industries, to renovate our physical infrastructure, to upgrade the skills of our people, and to protect our people against adversity. We must reject the negativism of so many conventional macroeconomic prescriptions. Less will not automatically become more; retrenchment will not automatically become expansion. We must restore to government the active and positive role that was outlined by the framers of our Constitution. We need to take pride in our collective capacity to solve problems through public policy. We need to initiate a new and dramatic national strategy designed to rebuild the American economy and distribute the fruits of economic growth fairly among our citizens. America deserves a program that is feasible in the present and appropriate for the future.

This book outlines such a program for Growth with Fairness. The American people must rediscover the path of economic productivity, competitiveness, and basic equity. We must consciously seek reinvigoration, turning our backs on years of neglect, mismanagement, and misplaced priorities. The Reagan administration's false hope that the "invisible hand'' of the market alone would solve our economic and social problems has contributed both to economic stagnation and to grave injustices in our society. But rebuilding the U.S. economy cannot be accomplished by smoke and mirrors, quick fixes, or public relations campaigns. The American people are prepared for a shift in national direction. We are not looking for miracles but for energetic, practical programs. We want a national policy that will regain control of our economic future and manage it responsibly in a way that restores our confidence that, by hard work, we will have a reasonable chance—as did the generations before us—to construct lives for ourselves and our children that are increasingly more prosperous, productive, and secure. The Democratic party must be prepared to embrace such programs with vigor if it is to justify its claim that it alone is the party of growth with fairness and thereby earn the support of the American people.

Chapter 2:

INDUSTRIAL DEVELOPMENT AND PUBLIC WORKS POLICY

A program for the renewal of America's productive potential must begin with a major and concerted effort to modernize our manufacturing industries and to rebuild our rapidly deteriorating infrastructure of roads, bridges, waste treatment, and water supply facilities. Our rate of investment for more than two decades has lagged behind that of our chief international competitors. It will not be sufficient for us merely to equal their current performance. To catch up, we must actually exceed their rates of investment for an extended period of time. We must find ways to manage, as efficiently as possible, these investments in manufacturing and public works and in the skills of our labor force. This is a formidable challenge, one that we as a nation cannot avoid. The invisible hand of the marketplace alone will not rebuild America's economy. We need a joint effort by our public and private sectors if America is to regain its capacity to produce goods and services competitively in world markets.

The Erosion of Competitiveness

During the past two decades our goods-producing industries have lost their competitive edge. Foreign manufacturers, often capitalizing on technologies that we invented and often helped by aggressive support from their own governments, have successfully invaded our domestic markets and have driven our goods out of most foreign markets with high-quality, reasonably priced, and innovative products. Our once-dominant machine tool industry is a typical example of the recent rapid deterioration of our ability to compete at home and abroad. As recently as 1977, U.S. firms exported more machine tools to the rest of the world than were imported into the United States. In 1985, on the other hand, the value of machine tool imports was more than four times that of our exports. Imports of machine tools had jumped from 16.7 percent of domestic consumption to 43.4 percent. America is now in the intolerable and unsustainable position of importing nearly double the value of the goods we are able to export and of financing the trade gap by massive borrowing from abroad. Our trade deficit now exceeds $160 billion per year. We have become, during the Reagan years, the world's largest debtor nation.

Meanwhile, the U.S. economy has increasingly become a service economy. After decades of steady growth, manufacturing employment stagnated in the 1970s at approximately 20 million persons, decreasing to 19 million by 1986. Between 1966 and 1986, the proportion of our labor force employed in manufacturing declined precipitously from over 30 percent to less than 20 percent. At the same time, employment in nongovernmental services—including wholesale and retail trade, real estate, and financial services—increased at an average annual rate of 3.5 percent, climbing from 47 percent of the work force in 1966 to 58 percent in 1986. The U.S. economy is moving toward the production of services, which have been demonstrated historically to travel less well than food products and manufactured goods. Real estate and retail trade, for example, two of the largest growth areas in our domestic economy, produce very little that is exportable. More and more of our people are working at jobs that do not produce goods or services that are competitive in world markets.

This shift of employment to the service sector is also increasing deprivation and insecurity among the working poor and diminishing the opportunities of the middle class. While the average gross hourly earnings in manufacturing in 1986 were $9.73, the equivalent wage in wholesale and retail trade was $6.02. While an average manufacturing worker was employed for 40.7 hours per week, an average retail trade em-

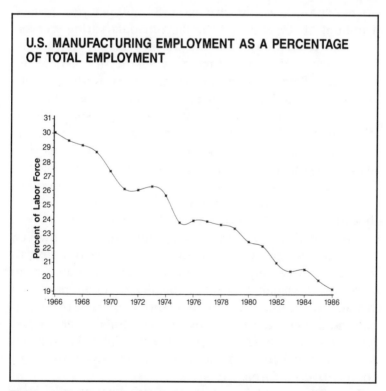

Figure 1: For two decades, American jobs have been shifting out of manufacturing and into services.

Source: *Economic Report of the President*, 1987, Table B-40.

ployee worked only 29.2 hours. A typical worker who was fired from the assembly line and was subsequently reemployed in a retail store suffered a 40 percent decline in hourly wages compounded by a 25 percent decrease in the number of hours worked, a total reduction of income of more than 50 percent. In addition to the reductions in income, many of the part-time, low-wage service jobs are without the health insurance and other benefits characteristic of the largely unionized manufacturing sector. Hence, the reduction in effective income is even larger. That typical manufacturing worker was not earning an outrageous or exorbitant income to begin with: $9.73 per hour translates into about $20,000 per year. A retail clerk making $6.02 per hour for less than 30 hours per week would earn about $9,000 per year. In fact, 4 million of the almost 12 million manufacturing workers displaced from their jobs in the last six years suffered at least a 25 percent reduction in income when they found new employment. Thus, as a nation, we have been trading in jobs at a decent wage for those that pay less than the poverty level.

America's competitive decline is therefore responsible for immense trade deficits and for large reductions in the income and living standards of working people. Why have our manufacturing industries lost ground to their major international competitors? Part of the explanation for the flood of imports into the United States is the starvation wage rates paid in Korea, Taiwan, and other Third World countries to which U.S. multinationals have exported American jobs. However, this is not the entire explanation for our lack of competitiveness. We also import substantial amounts of goods from Germany and Japan, where high-quality goods are produced at wage rates comparable to ours. Another part of the explanation has been the wildly overvalued dollar over the last few years. Yet the recent collapse of the dollar has not significantly reduced the trade deficit or improved America's competitive performance.

The fundamental explanation for the declining competitiveness of our manufacturing industries is a history of slow productivity growth. Competitiveness requires the creation

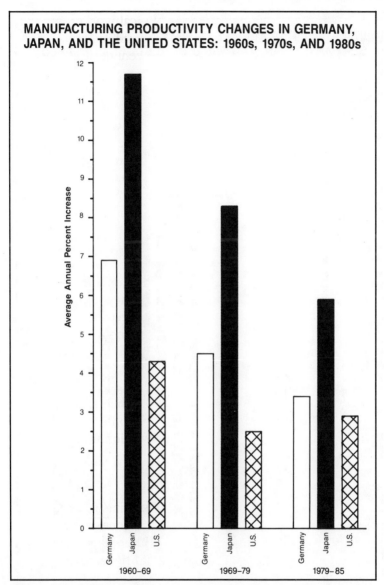

MANUFACTURING PRODUCTIVITY CHANGES IN GERMANY, JAPAN, AND THE UNITED STATES: 1960s, 1970s, AND 1980s

Figure 2: The rate of growth in manufacturing productivity has been much lower in the United States than in either Germany or Japan.

Source: *OECD Economic Outlook,* June 1986, Table 5.

Note: The figures for Japan in 1960–69 refer only to 1965–69 because comparable data were not available for earlier periods.

Source: *OECD Economic Outlook*, June 1986, Table 5.

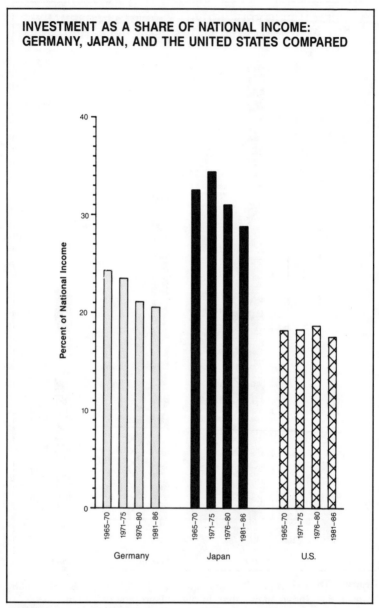

INVESTMENT AS A SHARE OF NATIONAL INCOME:
GERMANY, JAPAN, AND THE UNITED STATES COMPARED

Figure 3: The United States has consistently invested less of its income than either Germany or Japan.

Source: *OECD Economic Outlook*, December 1986, Table R-3; and *OECD Observer*, March 1986 and March 1987, "Annual Statistical Highlights."

of high-quality goods at reasonable prices. It also requires fair exchange rates and access to foreign markets. If our productivity—measured as the real value of output per unit of labor—does not continuously increase, then our goods will fall in price and quality behind those from other nations. In fact, the U.S. rate of manufacturing productivity is *not* rising as fast as that of our competitors. Between 1960 and 1984, productivity increased in Japan by an average of 7.7 percent per year, and in Germany by 3.7 percent. During this same period, productivity in the United States increased by an average of only 2.5 percent per year. With declining growth in productivity relative to our major competitors, it is no wonder that our manufacturing industries have been in decline.

Productivity increases in response to investment. Private investment in new plants and equipment, and public and private investment in physical infrastructure and in research and development promote competitiveness. Building more efficient factories, upgrading equipment, and providing better roads all allow firms to produce and market goods at a lower unit cost. Yet gross investment in the United States over the past two decades has averaged only 18 percent, compared with 22 percent in Germany and 32 percent in Japan. Moreover, investment in manufacturing has increased in the United States in real terms by only 2.9 percent per year, compared with an average growth rate of 4.6 percent annually in Japan. The proportion of national income spent on research and development for civilian purposes has remained substantially below that of our major international competitors. Over a period of years these cumulative differences have had a devastating effect on our industrial might.

Investments in industry, in public works, and in research and development are financed by our national savings. Yet U.S. net private domestic savings have declined significantly. Hypothetically, one could imagine a savings rate ample to finance all planned increases in private investment and to cover any revenue shortfall in government accounts. This is precisely the situation in Japan, where the savings rate exceeds 15 percent of national income, and in Germany, where the rate is just below 10 percent. Unfortunately, in recent years the opposite has occurred in the United States, where the savings rate has fallen below 5 percent. This, combined with the huge recent increase in the federal deficit, has established the preconditions for a dangerous capital shortage. Largely because of the government's imperative need to borrow, real interest rates have climbed. The hope is that a higher price for money will bring more of it into the financial market- place. Still, during the 1980s, the available supply of net domestic savings has remained below the amount required for net private domestic investment. The gap has been filled by a rising level of foreign penetration, which has necessi- tated interest rates much higher than those in other indus- trialized countries. According to Reagan's Council of Econom- ic Advisers, "In 1986, net capital inflows—and the associat- ed buildup of foreign claims on the United States—equaled one-half of U.S. net capital formation."

The implications are serious. Higher interest rates have raised the cost of capital, inhibiting efforts by U.S. firms to modernize and expand productive capacity. Higher capital costs mean that the internal rate of return on new investment goes down, making that investment less attractive to busi- ness managers. Some firms thus become less willing to in- vest, finding gradual obsolescence preferable to growth. Other firms, wishing to be dynamic and to modernize tech- nologically, nevertheless cannot obtain the necessary funds.

We are faced with a kind of catch-22 in financial markets. The U.S. budget and trade deficits require that U.S. interest rates remain high enough that foreign businesses and bankers will be willing to leave their money here, rather than take it to other financial markets. However, while these high in- terest rates keep us afloat on our international balance sheet, they raise the cost to the federal government of financing the budget deficits at those high interest rates: interest pay- ments on the national debt amounted to an astonishing $136 billion in 1986. Further, high interest rates make it difficult, if not impossible, for American industries to rebuild and compete in world markets with German or Japanese companies, which can borrow their investment capital at home less expensively. Yet if American interest rates were dramatically lowered, foreigners would cease financing the deficit and would do so quickly. Forty percent of the more than $780 billion in foreign financial assets in this country as of March 1987 were in U.S. government securities, almost all of which can be liquidated at a moments notice. In the most extreme scenario, without the ability to instantly increase our exports, we would have to immediately reduce our imports. Hence, we face the possibility that, as exchange values adjust and capital inflows decline, financial pressures will intensify, interest rates will soar, government will resort to inflation to pay its bills, foreign banks and corporations will buy U.S. assets at bargain prices, and a depressed American economy will lack the capacity to rejuvenate itself.

Available funds have not been channeled into productive private investments sufficiently in the last 20 years because of 1) corporate decisions to pay a larger proportion of their earnings in dividends and reduce the share that is reinvested in their own productive futures, 2) multinational corporate decisions to transfer production out of this country and into low-wage countries, and 3) bankers' and brokers' decisions to look for quick and easy returns in nonproductive sectors.

With a very low savings rate, the United States depends for its investment on corporations either retaining profits or borrowing. Steadily since the late 1950s, however, corporations have been retaining a smaller and smaller share of their after-tax profits, instead paying out larger and larger dividends—dividends which disproportionately benefit the less than 15 percent of American households that own any stock at all. In the 1960s, U.S. corporations paid out as dividends 47 percent of their after-tax earnings. During the Reagan presidency, that figure rose to 67 percent. Between 1981 and 1986, that amounted to more than $400 billion paid to shareholders rather than being reinvested in improved efficiency and enhanced competitiveness. U.S. firms have had, as a result, insufficient capital with which to modernize and improve productivity at the same rate as their foreign competitors.

It is thus no surprise that dependence on borrowing by American corporations has had to increase, raising the costs of production by adding interest expenses to the capital costs of modernization and expansion. Between 1981 and 1986, domestic borrowing for capital purchases increased from $155 billion to more than $500 billion. This was exacerbated by the flood of junk bonds issued by corporate raiders to finance their plundering of U.S. enterprises. With the inordinately high interest rates of the past six years, these increased costs alone have been sufficient to hamper the competitiveness of many U.S. producers, producers who are competing against foreign firms whose governments go out of their way to lower the costs of capital.

In addition to the wasting of profits by U.S. corporations and their increasing debt burden, multinational corporations and international banks have been investing substantial amounts of capital overseas rather than in the rebuilding of America's competitiveness. Between 1971 and 1981, massive amounts of capital were used to acquire private assets overseas, and since 1981, this bleeding of the American economy has continued. All told, more than $780 billion was used by U.S. multinationals for capital investment abroad between 1971 and 1986. This amounts to more than one-half of the total invested in new plants and equipment by all U.S. manufacturing corporations during this period. Imagine how much more productive and competitive our industries would be today had these funds been invested in rebuilding the U.S. economy rather than in acquiring assets abroad.

The quick payout of profits and the investment in overseas markets have been forced, in part, by the quarterly bottom line of Wall St. brokers and institutional investors interested in high rates of return in the immediate future. Unwilling to insist that investments be made with a view to the long term, they have continuously searched for better and easier ways to make a quick buck. Unwilling to invest in the modernization of America's productive structure, a project in which the payback will be measured in years rather than quarters, the money managers of America have abandoned their country. Trading in paper securities has risen dramatically during the Reagan "recovery." Our production of goods has been sabotaged, in large part, by bankers and brokers in search of immediate gain.

The private sector has let us down. The decline in manufacturing was not inevitable. Responsibility rests largely on the shoulders of America's leading investors, not on the backs of America's working men and women. Had industrialists, bankers, and brokers accepted their responsibility to ensure a prosperous future for America, our industries would be on the way to recovery already. The only sure way for the United States to reestablish a pattern of sustained growth—which is within our control and upon which we can depend—is to renew and reinvigorate our manufacturing industries.

The federal government has also let us down. Rather than play an active and vigorous role in maintaining the health and vitality of our manufacturing sector, it has largely neglected the problem and failed to find effective solutions. Historically, its approach to remedying shortfalls in investment has been to assume that if a little more money merely were placed in the right hands, those hands would put the money to the best use. Our nation's industrial policy rested primarily on periodic tax reductions for corporations and wealthy investors. During periods when the United States was the dominant producer in the world, we could afford to rely on such inefficient, unfocused, and indirect incentives. With dominance in the world economy came numerous attractive investment opportunities for those with a little more money. If many chose not to invest, that was tolerable because the United States enjoyed a substantial margin for error.

In the 1970s, insufficient alarm was raised over evidence of the decline of our traditional industries and the dramatic changes taking place in the world economy. The federal government's approach during that time to promoting economic development, in addition to the traditional reliance on undirected tax breaks, lay in two tracks. On one track, the government created and expanded a series of disparate programs intended to assist local economic development. Programs such as the Small Business Administration, the Economic Development Administration, and the Economic Development component of the Community Development Block Grants program were all designed to assist in the creation of new jobs. On a second track, the federal government stepped in to "bail out" major corporations when they were threatened with insolvency. Chrysler, Lockheed, and Conrail all were saved by federal intervention as an unstated policy of providing a "safety net" for large corporations gradually emerged. However, no coherent policy, program, or approach was developed during the 1970s to restore competitiveness to American industry.

Under the Reagan administration, even the minimal efforts undertaken within these two ad hoc tactics were abandoned, at least to the extent that Congress would allow it. Funding for the economic development agencies throughout the government has been decimated. Corporations, ranging from oil to airlines to banks, are now increasingly on their own when their creditors come calling. The government abstained from encouraging the rebuilding of America's industrial strength, lest it deviate from a dogmatic free market ideology.

The Reagan administration did continue to try to manipulate the corporate tax code. For example, the accelerated cost recovery system allowed capital equipment to be depreciated for tax purposes more rapidly than it actually decayed, resulting in an enormous tax break. Yet, careful research by Citizens for Tax Justice has shown that, while substantial benefits were received by America's corporations, they did little to stimulate investment. Indeed, there was simply no correlation between the value of the tax benefits received and the amount of new investments. For example, between 1981 and 1983, General Electric paid no taxes and actually received tax rebates of $283 million while reducing its investments by 15 percent. By contrast, Whirlpool paid taxes of almost $300 million while increasing its investments by 7 percent. Attempts to use the tax code to direct investment into modernization have faltered due to the difficulty of writing tax provisions that are general enough to be applicable to all, yet specific enough to be limited only to investments that improve competitiveness. Using tax benefits to induce capital formation has proven a hopelessly inefficient method of inducing corporate investments in the rebuilding of American industry.

The Reagan "recovery" has failed to restore American leadership in investment and productivity, the underpinnings for a successful return to competitiveness. While our rates of investment and productivity increases since 1983 have moved closer to Germany's levels, they are still well below Japan's. This "recovery" is insufficient for two reasons. First, much of the apparent improvement results from the bankruptcies of thousands of weaker companies, a statistical improvement with limited significance. It is easy to increase produc-

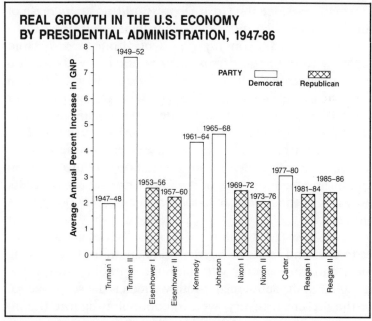

REAL GROWTH IN THE U.S. ECONOMY BY PRESIDENTIAL ADMINISTRATION, 1947-86

Figure 4: Growth in the U.S. economy has been much more sluggish in recent decades than previously. Furthermore, growth has been much stronger under Democratic than under Republican administrations.
Source: *Economic Report of the President*, 1987, Table B-11.

tivity by driving out of business those firms that have less capital to invest. The challenge for sustained growth is to find ways by which a wide array of our enterprises can be helped to modernize and survive. Second, recovery by mere catching up will not be nearly enough. After 20 years of relative stagnation in improvements to our productive capacity, the United States must substantially increase its level of investment in new plants and equipment, research and development, and physical infrastructure if we are to assure ourselves a future of competitiveness in world markets. Clearly, a more directed method of increasing investments is required.

The widely believed perception, promoted by the White House, that Reagan's policies brought this country back to economic health is belied by the facts. The Reagan formula for economic recovery brought about the deepest recession, the highest rate of unemployment, the largest number of business failures since the Great Depression, and an increase of the federal debt by more than $1 trillion. From the depths of 1982, the U.S. economy experienced one year of rapid recovery from the doldrums and a period of steady but unspectacular growth since. Between 1981 and 1986, the real value of U.S. goods and services grew at an annual rate of 2.3 percent. This is even slightly less than during the Carter years, 1977–81, which the public remembers as a time of economic sluggishness. The net increase in employment in the first six years of the Reagan administration was also less than that during the four years of the Carter presidency. By 1986, fully half of the American labor force earned $11,000 or less annually.

We are now faced with three choices. We can allow America to drift and living standards gradually to decline, leaving more and more people without hope, without a future. Or, recognizing the substantial inequity which is the consequence of the present recovery, we can continue to ignore the inherent fragility of the debt-ridden Reagan economy and construct an elaborate new array of social welfare programs to redistribute income from those who prosper to those who do not. Or we can intervene vigorously in the market economy to encourage and prod investments back to manufacturing and industrial revitalization, while insuring the individual well-being that Americans have come to accept as part of their heritage. The United States has had a historic commitment to an expanding economy capable of disseminating its benefits throughout our citizenry. The Growth with Fairness proposals for an industrial development and public works policy specify the means by which this commitment can and should be met.

The Growth with Fairness program calls for three initiatives directly linked to the renewal of our industrial capacity: 1) the creation of an Industrial Development Bank, chartered to invest in the modernization and expansion of manufacturing industries; 2) the adoption of a set of antiraiding policies to protect corporate managers from defensive preoccupation with the quarterly bottom line, which diminishes their ability to contemplate the investments required for long-term growth; and 3) a substantial increase in the federal commitment to repairing, rehabilitating, and expanding the physical infrastructure of our country, without which no strategy for economic development will succeed.

These three initiatives constitute an industrial development and public works policy that will put America back on the road to domestic prosperity and international competitiveness. By channeling increased investment into our manufacturing industries, by decreasing the incentives for the continuing waste of talent and resources in merger mania, by rebuilding the physical underpinnings of our economic growth, and by liberating the states to pursue innovative efforts in support of job creation, this program will reverse the pernicious drift of recent years. With this industrial development policy in place, American firms and American workers will produce high-quality products at competitive prices once again.

Establishing an Industrial Development Bank

America needs an industrial development policy that encourages the manufacture of those goods which the United

States can produce and sell successfully in world markets and of which it ought to be a major producer for its own domestic consumption. Previous calls for an industrial policy in America have faltered on the distinction between predicting "winners" and rescuing "losers." An effective policy must recognize that many American industries can be winners— including some of the traditional "sunset" industries, such as automobiles—if sufficient resources are devoted to modernization and training. As economists Barry Bluestone and Bennett Harrison recommend in their pioneering study, *The Deindustrialization of America*, only a broad and diverse set of efforts will rebuild American competitiveness and prosperity. Even within disappearing industries, there are special niches in which American firms can find profitable investments. The job of a new industrial policy is to identify industries and niches that, with the proper period of rebuilding, can be competitive at home and abroad.

The 1000 largest U.S. manufacturers presently spend between $75 and $100 billion per year on new plants and equipment; the total for all manufacturers is between $100 and $150 billion. This spending ranges from the replacement of obsolete machinery to the building of entirely new production facilities. Two-thirds of the 23 member countries in the Organization for Economic Cooperation and Development (OECD) spend more as a share of gross domestic product (GDP) than does the United States on investments in machinery and equipment.

In many areas, industry groups have recently recognized the need to take a coordinated approach to the future. For example, several major producers of machine tools and manufactured goods have formed the National Center for Manufacturing Sciences with the aim of raising $500 million with which to sponsor a wide-ranging program of research and development. A substantial number of computer-dependent firms have joined the Microelectronics and Computer Technology Corporation to develop applications for the power of modern computing that will enhance American productivity. Less than a year after commencing its research operations, MCC delivered its first product, Proteus, a computer program that functions to both simulate and assist the operations of professionals in tasks ranging from medical diagnosis to analysis of mechanical faults in engines. However, despite these hopeful beginnings, to modernize and expand production facilities will require substantial new investments with a relatively long payback period.

Investments will be needed to bring the full advantages of American-created technologies into the workplace. The United States lags substantially behind its European and Japanese competitors in the uses of computer-integrated management systems, which allow production efficiency to be greatly increased. We lag behind in our uses of robotics, by which mechanical devices can assemble products much more inexpensively and can handle dangerous toxins more safely. We lag behind in the introduction of energy efficiency into many of our major production processes. We must eliminate the gaps between our processes of production and those of our major competitors if the United States is to restore its competitiveness at home and abroad. The aim of our policy must be to provide all those firms that are willing to make a commitment to modernization the opportunity and the means to do so.

Industrial modernization on a national scale depends on the availability of substantial amounts of capital from lenders and investors willing to undertake substantial risks with a relatively long time horizon. In most countries, some special facility for financing industrial development is established when the nation's economy as a whole requires reinvigoration. Marshall Plan aid to Western Europe served this purpose after World War II, providing large amounts of capital as grants or low-interest loans and thus making possible investment in the much-needed reconstruction of European industrial capacity. The Koreas and Brazils of this world have become serious industrial competitors largely through the efficient and effective operations of their industrial development banks, including the Korea Development Bank, the Korean Small and Medium Industry Bank, and the Brazilian National Bank for Economic Development.

The federal government in this country too has a distinguished history of stimulating job creation by assisting in the financing of private enterprise. For example, the Bank of the United States was established by Alexander Hamilton during Washington's presidency, and the Reconstruction Finance Corporation was initiated by President Hoover and then greatly expanded by President Roosevelt as one of the principal instruments used to lift America out of the Great Depression. Needed now is an innovative approach to carry on that tradition.

Thus, the Growth with Fairness program calls for the creation of an industrial development bank chartered to increase new investments in plants and equipment. Capital for the IDB would be provided initially by the U.S. Treasury at $10 billion per year. Funding would be phased out within approximately five years as the Bank achieved self-financing capability. The Bank would use its capital to take minority equity positions in firms receiving assistance in the creation of new, or the modernization of existing, facilities. These would not be investments with an immediate payoff. The IDB's purpose would be to finance those enhancements to our industrial capacity that are most likely to improve the competitiveness of our industries and our nation, not to seek the quickest profits for the sake of its own balance sheet.

While $10 billion per year in new investment capital is no panacea for American industry, it could make a substantial difference. Much of the $100 billion invested by U.S. manufacturing firms in 1986 in new plants and equipment was financed by borrowing. Each $10 billion borrowed generates less than $10 billion in new investments, as a part of the fund must be reserved to help repay the principal and interest on the loan. By one reliable estimate, under current credit conditions, this reduces the value of the borrowing by 50 percent. In other words, an additional $10 billion in equity capital available from the IDB would generate roughly the same amount of real investment activity as $20 billion from the financial markets where U.S. firms raised most of their investment capital in 1986. Hence, a $10 billion addition of equity capital from the IDB would increase investment by American manufacturing firms more than would the same amount provided by commercial loans. This is clearly the kind of increase in investment that is required if American industry is to regain its competitive edge.

Administered as a bank with manufacturing job creation as its goal, the IDB would serve as a continuing agency to assist the private sector in circumventing the very short time horizons of contemporary U.S. capital markets. In taking equity in return for its financing, the Bank would not get into the business of running business enterprises. Restrictions on the share of corporate equity that may be held by the Bank would be required. In addition, the IDB would have to be chartered in such a way as to insulate its decisions, as much as possible, from the political demands of particular interests. This has been common practice with many of the federal government's credit-granting agencies and institutions. It also applies in different ways to such diverse bodies as the Federal Reserve Board and the International Trade Commission.

The Bank would offer to finance the gap between the level of expenditures needed to modernize or expand production facilities in targeted industrial sectors and the level of financing available from the private sector. Such gap financing would leverage funds from the private sector, encouraging private investors who otherwise would place their funds in financial or real estate speculation to instead invest productively in rebuilding American industry.

The principal criteria for industries receiving government assistance would be 1) their job-creating potential, 2) their potential technological edge in world markets in both product and production process, and 3) the requirements of national defense and economic security. Among others, this would include automobiles, steel, machine tools and capital goods equipment, semiconductors, petroleum refining, computers, telecommunications equipment, and scientific instruments. Of course, this is but a brief illustrative list, not intended to be inclusive of the wide range of products and industries that—with careful planning, vigilant management, and assistance from the IDB—might be made competitive.

Financing would depend on the presentation of a 5- to 10-year business plan demonstrating the competitiveness and the job-creating potential of the proposed investment. Instead of granting the blank check typically issued under previous approaches to stimulating industrial investment, the IDB would consider investing only when presented with specific plans for acquisition of new equipment, construction of new facilities, improvement of job training, or other activities directly related to modernizing of our capacity for production. If the Bank chose to finance the project, the funds would be used to purchase newly issued shares in the requesting company, with the provision that the shares would not be traded by the IDB for a period of five years. The Bank's reliance on equity rather than credit would avoid saddling corporations with additional debt, the repayment of which often strangles successful efforts to build for the future. With an equity investment, management would be freed to do what they should be doing: figuring out the best way to produce high-quality goods at competitive prices. The returns on the investment would come when the investment became profitable. Hence, the IDB's method of financing would avoid either burdening the corporation with additional debt or subjecting corporate management to additional pressure to respond to short-term demands for profitability.

The IDB would be investing in the modernization of American industry. It would choose its investments carefully, as does any bank, with the expectation of a reasonable rate of return over time. Of course, no investment is a guaranteed success. Some assistance may go to firms that fail, for one reason or another. Yet careful assessments of the financing proposals that are submitted to the Bank ought to allow the Bank's investment officers to predict with reasonable confidence the liklihood of success of any given venture. Under these circumstances, the IDB should be self-financing after approximately five-years, with the equity holdings and returns on those holdings constituting its assets. Had the United States such a Bank in 1979 when the Chrysler Corporation sought federal assistance, and had the Bank extended financial assistance through the purchase of new equity instead of through loan guarantees, the Bank would now have assets worth more than $30 billion in return for its initial investment of $1.5 billion. It would already be quite well prepared to assist U.S. manufacturers in rebuilding America's manufacturing base for the future.

To encourage the states to share responsibility for, and participate as partners in, the reindustrialization of America, the IDB would also channel funds for smaller investments to state industrial development banks for them to administer. This would enable the states to encourage job creation by small and medium-size businesses, as long as they follow the same guidelines that would govern the federal bank.

Indeed, the policies of the Industrial Development Bank ought to support a revival of our tradition of cooperative federalism. Recent experience has demonstrated the innovative potential of our state governments in finding ways to create jobs in productive, competitive businesses. Traditional reliance upon targeted tax incentives and the creation of industrial parks is being supplemented by novel approaches to financing future development. Loan guarantees, such as those issued by the New Jersey Economic Developemnt Authority, are being used increasingly to encourage private lenders to invest in projects in which the immediate return is lower than might be realized elsewhere. Direct loans from state industrial development agencies, such as the Kentucky Industrial Development Finance Authority, often are funded from revolving loan funds capitalized by state bond issues. More than 10 states have created equity or venture capital corporations, with the authority to invest directly in new or expanding operations. In virtually every state, governors and legislatures are anxious to encourage healthy economic development. Assisting a local bakery or an emerging manufacturer of computer chips is a task best handled at the state, not federal, level.

Vigorous action by the states is essential to a future of sustained growth. State action, however, cannot be sufficient. States must operate within rules established by the federal government, including those covering labor-management relations, interstate commerce, and foreign trade. Moreover, states have more limited financial resources than the federal government, and hence, they often fall short on large projects. Without strong federal action, states find themselves in a scramble to give away land and tax breaks as they compete against one another to attract large, new investments. This bidding up of the incentives offered for new investments channels resources away from the essential tasks of reconstructing our economy and society. Hence, the federal government must undertake positive steps to promote growth and, at the same time, maintain a sufficiently strict regulatory framework to insure that state actions are constructive and not mutually destructive. The program for Growth with Fairness would apportion responsibilities efficiently, giving the federal government primary obligation for overall macroeconomic conditions and for industrial development nationwide.

Discouraging Corporate Raiding

In U.S. economic history the Reagan years will be regarded as the era of "greenmail" and corporate piracy. With the benign acquiescence of the federal government, some of the most efficient U.S. corporations have become the targets of financial predators bent on bidding up the stock prices of these companies. These predators either retired from the fray after pocketing millions in greenmail as ransom for for their piracy or actually took control of their victims by issuing high-risk junk bonds that saddled the surviving corporation with enormous burdens of debt. When the predators were successful, they often undertook to milk the target company of its assets for short-term profits or to sell off units to raise cash to ease the burden of debt created by their takeover strategies. The energies of the managers of the target firms, whether or not they successfully resisted the hostile takeovers, were diverted from the serious business of production and marketing to defensive and unproductive legal and financial maneuvers. And whatever the outcome, quick fortunes have been made by investment bankers, legal firms, and accounting companies retained by the predators and their intended victims; such fortunes have come from funds that could have been better spent on research, product development, expansion of markets, employee training, and modernization of facilities.

Most corporate raiders have no experience, expertise, or even interest in industrial management. Specialists in financial manipulation, they are more interested in making a fast killing than in patiently building the strength of productive enterprises. This orgy of hostile corporate takeovers, which involved an estimated $330 billion of U.S. corporate assets during the first four Reagan years, has contributed literally nothing to U.S. industrial efficiency or to our international competitiveness. Instead, it has weakened our companies by loading them with heavy debts that reduce their ability either

---

THE RAID ON BEATRICE FOODS

The *New York Times* magazine section of Sunday, September 6, 1987, reports the bizarre story of the seizure and dismemberment of Beatrice Foods. The article is appropriately titled, "Shaking Billions from the Beatrice Money Tree." A group of Wall Street manipulators gained control of the corporation by a leveraged buy-out, systematically sold off its assets, and pocketed literally billions of dollars in profits. The initiators of the scheme paid themselves "fees" of $45 million, the firm that sold the junk bonds charged $86 million for its services, and three brokerage firms engaged as "consultants" walked off with $15 million, $8 million, and $8 million, respectively. Six executives of Beatrice Foods were bought off for $22 million, presumably for agreeing not to resist the takeover. Nearly $3.5 billion in profits were realized by the instigators of the raiding party. Not a penny of wealth was created, nor was productive efficiency or competitiveness improved.

These enormous gains from predatory, nonproductive financial manipulations are apparently legal, an example of the distorted system of economic rewards prompted by the atmosphere of unregulated greed that has been the hallmark of the Reagan years.

---

to raise capital or to use their earnings for badly needed long-term investments in new or improved plants and equipment.

Contrary to the view of apologists for corporate raiding, modern corporate enterprises are not merely financial assets to be bought and sold at whim. They are complex associations of managers, skilled workers of many kinds, suppliers, dealers, and the communities that depend on them, all of whose common interests are tied to the competitive success of the enterprise. Corporate raiding disrupts and often destroys these networks, themselves a form of "social capital" that takes many years to build. In Japan, our most prominent competitor, corporate raiding is an unheard-of practice. The Japanese build the long-term strength and competitiveness of their firms by investing in the skills and commitment of their management teams and their workers, and by emphasizing the long-run expansion of market shares rather than the quarterly bottom line. This used to be the practice of U.S. firms in the heyday of our industrial supremacy.

The serious business of rebuilding the international competitiveness of U.S. industry is incompatible with an industrial environment in which the quarterly bottom line must take precedence over the long-term efficiency and profitability of the firm, and in which corporate managers must waste their energies on defensive maneuvers rather than dedicate themselves to the constructive tasks of designing, producing, and marketing high-quality goods at reasonable prices. U.S. corporate managers are certainly not paragons of efficiency. There have been many oversights, abuses, and lost opportunities in recent years that have reduced our industrial competitiveness for which they cannot avoid responsibility. Nevertheless, our industrial managers overall have tremendous capabilities that must be enlisted in the campaign to renew the effectiveness of our industry. For this to happen, however, they must be relieved of the pernicious threats and unproductive diversions of energy brought about by the corporate raiders.

The federal government cannot afford to stand aside and allow these destructive takeover practices to continue. Instead, it should, as fellow Cornell faculty member William F. Whyte has proposed in recent testimony to Congress, take positive measures to put an end to the hijacking of legitimate U.S. businesses by financial pirates. The following measures, part of this plan for Growth with Fairness, would bring these destructive practices under control:

- Eliminate the pretax deduction of interest payments on junk bonds. This is an unwarranted subsidy to the predators at the expense of the U.S. taxpayers and a major incentive for corporate raiders. This change in the tax laws would not affect friendly mergers that are implemented by exchanges of stock.
- Revise the tax laws to prevent acquiring firms from arbitrarily writing up the paper value of the capital assets of target companies, inflating their capital depreciation allowances, and thereby avoiding large sums in taxes.
- Direct the Securities and Exchange Commission (SEC) and the Treasury to tighten requirements for issuing the high-risk junk bonds that have financed most hostile takeovers.
- Require a mandatory waiting period of at least 120 days between the announcement of a takeover project and the time at which it can be consummated. This will deprive predators of the tactical advantage of surprise and allow management, workers, and communities time in which to mobilize in defense of their legitimate interests.

Rehabilitating Our Physical Infrastructure

No effort to reindustrialize America can succeed unless our crumbling infrastructure is put back in working order. One of the central responsibilities of government is to maintain the physical infrastructure in a condition that allows growth with fairness to proceed on a solid foundation. Without adequate highways and inland waterways, the transportation of intermediate goods needed by producers and of final goods for sale to the public will prove an obstacle to our renewed industrial strength. Without improved port facilities, the business of exporting goods will be held up by bottlenecks in transit. Without a better capacity to keep our water supplies clean, industrial expansion will jeopardize our environment and our health. Indeed, much of America's physical infrastructure, from our railways and subways to our school buildings and libraries, is crucial to our economic vitality.

From the early days of the Republic, the federal government has recognized the need and accepted the responsibility to assist in creating and maintaining the physical capital required for our prosperity. In the 1820s, the Army Corps of Engineers undertook the building of harbors and inland waterways. In the 1830s, the National Road was constructed, linking Washington to Ohio. From the 1840s through the 1870s, the federal government offered land grants to encourage construction of railroads.

In the twentieth century, the federal role has expanded in an evolving partnership with the states. In 1902, the Department of Interior's Bureau of Reclamation began building the first of more than 700 dams to harness the nation's water resources. Fourteen years later, the federal government offered to finance 50 percent of the construction costs for state and local road systems. The Tennessee Valley Authority was created in 1933 to provide water and energy resources for that region, while in 1937 the Farmers' Home Administration began to develop water systems in rural areas. In 1956, the Highway Trust Fund was established to finance 90 percent of the cost of completing the interstate highway system. In the following year, federal grants to finance up to 30 percent of the cost of new wastewater treatment facilities were authorized. Through these and innumerable other efforts, the United States entered the 1960s with one of the best-developed physical infrastructures in the world.

Building and maintaining durable structures costs substantial amounts of money. However, over the last two decades, the proportion of our national income that was spent on physical capital was cut in half. By 1980, a crisis had emerged due to our government's failure to spend enough on maintaining our existing transportation networks, water treatment systems, and other infrastructure systems. Bridges falling, subway ceilings collapsing, wastewater treatment plants unable to handle additional flow, air traffic control systems operating with outdated equipment—these were but the most visible signs of decay. In 1983, the Federal Highway Administration rated the condition of more than half of all roads and highways in the nation less than good. The sorry state of America's physical capital stock was assessed most comprehensively and brought to the attention of the country in economists Pat Choate and Susan Walter's 1981 analysis, *America in Ruins.*

Investment in our physical capital is vital to our economic recovery. A Department of Transportation study done in 1983 predicted that the deteriorating condition of the nation's highways alone would reduce labor productivity in manufacturing by 2.7 percent and the GNP by 3.2 percent in 1995. At the same time, a Department of Commerce survey found that more than 50 percent of the wastewater treatment facilities in the country were already operating at a level that would preclude the creation of any additional industrial users.

Yet during the Reagan period, expenditures on physical resources fell by a full 1 percent of GNP—from 10.5 percent of federal spending to 5.9 percent, a decrease equivalent to more than $45 billion per year. The administration sought to eliminate assistance to local areas, through the Community Development Block grants, for physical improvements. It attempted to eliminate assistance to mass transit systems despite their obviously critical role in allowing congested urban areas to continue to function as viable economic and social units. And it sought to reduce assistance to localities for the construction of wastewater treatment facilities and for airports. Across the board, the Reagan administration pursued its false sense of economy. The potentially disastrous condition of our physical capital stock is one more legacy of neglect bestowed by the Reagan administration on future generations. This penny-wise but disastrous decline in federal spending on the most basic of needs for industrial and community development must be emphatically reversed.

In spite of determined resistance from Congress, which muted the most draconian of the administration's proposals, the Reagan administration succeeded in substantially reducing the federal commitment to public works. Even the battles waged at the beginning of the 100th Congress in 1987, when the president vetoed congressional authorizations for clean water and for highway and mass transit assistance, were largely battles to maintain funding at existing levels. For example, the mass transit bill, which authorized $13 billion in spending spread over five years, only maintained funding at

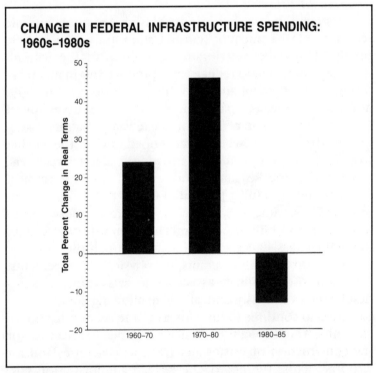

CHANGE IN FEDERAL INFRASTRUCTURE SPENDING: 1960s–1980s

Figure 5: For the first time in two decades, the real value of federal spending on public works has declined during the 1980s.
Source: Congressional Budget Office, *The Federal Budget for Public Works Infrastructure*, July 1985, p. 1.

its 1986 level, a level which, in real terms, was 30 percent less than it had been in 1981. Between 1980 and 1985, federal spending on seven major infrastructural systems (highways, aviation, mass transit, wastewater treatment, water resources, water supply, and railroads) declined in real terms by 13 percent. This decrease contrasted with a 24 percent real increase in the 1960s and a 46 percent real increase in the 1970s. Even with these increases over the previous two decades, our nation's bridges, highways, airports, and water treatment plants are in a weakened condition. To decrease spending in the face of these clear and present perils is the most dangerous and hypocritical kind of economizing.

A 1983 study by the Associated General Contractors of America estimated that approximately $3 trillion would be required by the year 2000 to repair, rehabilitate, maintain, and expand our physical infrastructure. *Hard Choices*, the National Advisory Committee report to the Joint Economic Committee of Congress in February 1984, estimated that more than $1 trillion would be needed for just five major components of our national network of public works. Even with a conservative estimate of $1.5 to $2.0 trillion in needed expenditures, current efforts by federal, state, and local government could be expected to provide only about half that amount. The shortfall, approximately $40 to $50 billion per year, must be provided by public and private sources if we are to have the physical capacity to support an industrial and economic renewal.

The need for an additional $40 to $50 billion per year in public spending on physical capital cannot and should not be met entirely by the federal government. The partnership between federal and state levels of government for the construction and maintenance of our physical infrastructure is a sound one, which must be maintained. But while many states have begun to step into the void left by the federal government, some have not. Overall, increases in state funding of public works during the 1980s have failed to match federal decreases. Proposals for innovative financing of new construction, for increased user fees in certain areas, and for improved management and auditing of the projects should be pursued further to ensure that public expenditures buy as much as possible. However, these are unlikely to significantly reduce the total level of federal expenditure required to bring our country's physical infrastructure back into a reasonable state of repair.

Hence, this program for Growth with Fairness calls for a $25 billion per year increase in federal spending on public works to rehabilitate our decaying physical infrastructure of roads, bridges, and waste treatment and water supply systems. This would increase public works' share of the federal budget to 8.6 percent, or 2 percent of GNP—still below its 1981 level. It would allow us to turn immediately to the reconstruction of an air traffic control system that once was the envy of the world. It would allow us to renew a commitment to mass transit and clean water, both of which are vital if our economic resurgence is to be consistent with a sane environmental policy. It would allow us to undertake a major program to reconstruct our port facilities so that they can serve to encourage, rather than discourage, the export of our products. And it would allow us to repair and rebuild the bridges and roadways that link the commerce of this country in a single coherent fabric.

This major expansion of our public works efforts would not only provide the necessary underpinning for our industrial rejuvenation, but would contribute directly to reducing unemployment as well. Extrapolating from a 1984 study done by Data Resources Inc., which evaluated the impact of a $10 billion per year increase in public works spending, we can anticipate that a $25 billion per year increase would produce approximately 4 million jobs, including more than 400,000 in manufacturing industries. That we are building the solid foundation for our future prosperity while creating employment immediately makes this a most worthwhile increase in federal spending.

Conclusion

Reinvigorated American industrial development requires a

creative partnership between public and private sectors. It demands that the government perform the tasks proper to its domain and that it give appropriate encouragement to business success. The Reagan free market policies stripped from government the ability to contribute the essential physical underpinnings of economic growth and left business investment without direction. They allowed corporate raiders and financial manipulators to plunder American firms for their own selfish, short-term interests. By contrast, this industrial development and public works policy calls for a return to government leadership. The public sector must commit itself to rebuilding the decaying infrastructure necessary to all production, and it must help private businesses find capital on reasonable terms to insure the modernization that is essential to the restoration of our industrial competitiveness.

While this industrial development and public works policy stands as the centerpiece of the Growth with Fairness program to rebuild America, it cannot stand alone. The measures presented in this chapter will serve little purpose if our hopes for sustainable growth are not reconciled with the opportunities and threats presented by the international economy. Neither industrial development nor trade policies will generate sufficient growth or true fairness unless they are complemented by measures to help individuals achieve their full productive potential. Together industrial development, trade, and fairness policies must be undertaken in a fiscally responsible manner, a manner in which the pattern of generating federal revenues and disbursing expenditures itself encourages growth with fairness. We must strive to unite the power of business, labor, and government together in an effort to reclaim the American tradition for our time. Without these policies, we shall remain less than we can be.

Chapter 3:

INTERNATIONAL TRADE POLICY

Any program for the renewal of America's economic prosperity will fail unless it includes, as an integral component, a coherent set of policies to deal with the threats and the opportunities presented by the world economy. A program for growth with fairness must confront directly our enormous trade deficit, which gives foreign governments and foreign investors the power to determine our economic future. It must avoid the extremist excesses of both those who would have us place our blind faith in the magic of free trade and those who would have us build a wall of barriers at America's borders. Fortunately, there is an alternative that is neither defeatist nor defensive: we must seize the initiative and insist that our international trade policy serve our national interest by supporting our economic growth, not stifling it.

Nations export those goods that they have in abundance and produce efficiently; they import those goods that they lack or can obtain from others at a higher quality or lower price. When operating in balance, the entire system of world exchanges offers to owners, managers, and workers the prospect of expanded markets for sales and, therefore, gives them a strong reason to continue producing. In turn, it offers to consumers a wider selection of goods available for purchase. As long as a rough balance is maintained between our exports and imports, America can anticipate the sustained domestic economic growth that is consistent with dynamic international trade, and our producers and our consumers can expect a growing opportunity to work and to enjoy the fruits of their labor. In recent years, however, that balance has been destroyed. America is now running persistent and unsupportable trade deficits. We must confront the challenges of a debtor nation trying to rebuild.

Key US Industries Decline in Market Shares

in the U.S. Market	1960	1970	1985
Automobiles	96%	83%	79%
Steel	96%	86%	75%
Consumer Electronics	94%	68%	39%
Metal-Forming Machine Tools	97%	93%	78%
Textile Machinery	93%	67%	59%

in World Markets:	1962	1970	1985
Motor Vehicles	23%	18%	7%
Aircraft	71%	67%	50%
Telecommunications Equipment	29%	15%	15%
Metal Working Machinery	33%	17%	10%
Agricultural Machinery	40%	30%	20%

Source: *"The Reindustrialization of America,"* Business Week, *Special Issue, June 30, 1980, p. 60; The Council on Economic Priorities, The Costs and Consequences of Reagan's Military Buildup, 1982, Table I; and United Nations,* International Trade Statistics Yearbook, *1985.*

To reverse America's declining position in world markets will require us both to regain equilibrium in our international accounts in the short-term and to restore our capacity for competitive production in the medium-term. To accomplish these tasks, the Growth with Fairness program calls for measures that address three basic problems: 1) the pernicious policies pursued by certain other countries, which give them discriminatory advantages in their competition with American producers; 2) the perverse and counterproductive policies pursued by the U.S. government, which lead to the export of American jobs; and 3) the lack of competitiveness of many leading American industries as a result of years of neglect both by management and government. The first two problems demand our attention if we are to balance our international books and restore fairness to our international trade. The third problem stands as the critical constraint on our ability to maintain growth and prosperity in the future. A vigorous and effective trade policy can contribute much to the solution of our current economic difficulties. The history of world trade relations shows that such a policy has been commonly practiced. It is now needed urgently.

Trade Policy and the National Interest

Most Americans believe that the expansion of world trade, and a prominent U.S. role in that trade, is good for America and good for the world. There is solid historical experience to support that belief. The impressive economic growth of the United States and the world economy after World War II, continuing until the late 1960s, was associated with a steady expansion in world trade. Between 1946 and 1971, the U.S. economy grew at an average annual rate of 3.3 percent; during this same period, exports grew at a rate of 3.9 percent, accounting for more than 7 percent of the U.S. GNP by 1971. At the same time, the world economy as a whole was growing at an average annual rate of 3.7 percent while world exports were growing by 5.7 percent. Growth in trade and growth in the productive capacities of the United States and the world economy worked together during this period in a mutually reinforcing manner.

However, we must read the lessons of this period carefully. Expanded trade was accompanied by persistent efforts by all major trading countries to ensure that their own producers and workers benefited from the opportunities presented by the world economy. The world trade system of the 1950s and 1960s, which allowed and encouraged this impressive economic momentum, was not a free trade system. It was a more multilateral and liberal system than the "beggar thy neighbor" world of the 1930s. Instead of each country relying primarily on bilateral trade agreements with other nations, most countries accepted the principle of granting equal access to all trade partners. In this way, any special benefit extended to one nation was automatically extended to others. Instead of each country trying to isolate its economy from the rest of the world through a broad and highly restrictive set of tariffs and quotas, the postwar world witnessed a reduction in quotas and tariff levels.

Yet even in this liberal trading system, every country retained the right to balance its national interests against the dictates of the world market. Whether for domestic rebuilding or for national security, every country in the world exercised some restraint on its openness to participation in the world economy.

Japan's Ministry for International Trade and Industry (MITI), widely regarded as a critical factor in Japan's economic miracle, organized from the beginning a concerted strategy for Japanese success in international markets. This campaign, begun in earnest in 1950, focused public and private sector assistance and collaboration on those industries targeted for export growth. At the same time, imports of agricultural and consumer goods were discouraged through a combination of informal and formal arrangements. The United States did not resist these mercantilist efforts to exclude foreign products, including American, from the Japanese domestic market and to expand Japan's participation in world trade. We rightly encouraged them in the belief that these measures would help to create a strong economy in a country that has allied itself loyally with the United States since World War II.

Japan was not alone in taking a vigorous and somewhat nationalistic approach to world trade after World War II. Our Western European friends also sought to increase their prosperity and solidify their reconstruction after the war by deliberate intervention in trade relations. As early as 1950, France, Germany, Belgium, the Netherlands, and Luxembourg formed the European Coal and Steel Community, precursor to the European Economic Community (EEC). The common tariff arrangements adopted by the European communities, both as they were originally designed and as they have developed since the 1950s, served to reduce the possibility of U.S. manufacturing and agricultural exports to Europe, while allowing the Europeans themselves to reestablish and expand their own industries. Here again the United States did not resist. We recognized that it was important for our European friends and allies to have the security that can only come from a productive economy capable of generating wealth in a competitive world.

Our partners were not alone in believing that prudent national restrictions on trade were an important element of a sensible world trading system. From the very beginning of the postwar period, the United States held firmly to the belief that the benefits of free trade had to be reconciled with the national interest in a strong economy. Divided after the 1946 elections between a Democratic administration and a Republican Congress, the U.S. government was nonetheless united in that view. As Jacob Viner, the distinguished conservative economist, observed in 1951:

> Only the traditional free trader can deal with the problem of the desirable level of trade barriers as a clear-cut question of principle. . . . The free trader objects to trade barriers both as obstacles to international specialization of production in accordance with comparative national advantages for production, and as sources of international friction.

> But there are few free traders in the present-day
> world, no one pays any attention to their views,
> and no person in authority anywhere advocates
> free trade.

In proposing a draft charter for the International Trade Organization, which was to govern postwar trade relations, President Truman and the State Department, according to Viner, gave "assurances that no reduction of duty will be made which would involve 'serious injury' to any American industry." Even quotas, a more drastic tool for regulating international trade than tariffs, were recognized as useful under limited circumstances. The draft charter proposed that they be allowed "as supplements to domestic crop-restriction or price-support or industrial development programs."

Clearly, from the outset of the postwar era and during the period when the ITO was proposed and the General Agreement on Tariffs and Trade (GATT) was accepted, the United States was committed to a system of liberalized trade but allowed for some protection when it was essential to our national economic and security interests. This historical truth is sometimes obscured by the fact that for much of the first two decades following the war, the era of the "dollar gap," the U.S. national interest was best served by the most open arrangements possible because our economy was such an efficient producer of such a wide range of goods. At a time when U.S. goods were able to meet or beat the competition in quality and cost, the United States served its own interests and those of the world by lowering its trade barriers and seeking to get others to lower theirs. During this period, the United States enjoyed trade surpluses with virtually every part of the world, and it financed the trade deficits of other countries with aid and investment flowing from the U.S. capital surplus.

By the late 1960s, however, the world economy had changed. Our efforts to assist in rebuilding Western Europe and Japan had succeeded beyond all expectations. While our trading partners had invested heavily in the construction of new production facilities and in the most recent technologies, U.S. industries lagged behind. Hence, by the second half of the 1960s, the U.S. economy was growing at a rate of 3 percent per year, while the European communities were averaging 4.5 percent, and Japan was growing at an annual rate of more than 11 percent. These higher growth rates of our trading partners reflected in large part their higher growth rates in manufacturing productivity.

As a result of these shifting patterns of productivity and trade, many of the most profitable investment opportunities in the world were appearing in countries other than the United States. The phenomenal growth of the Eurodollar market—a network of investment funds available outside the United States, which grew from $14 billion in 1964 to $215 billion in 1974— signaled the view of many corporations with

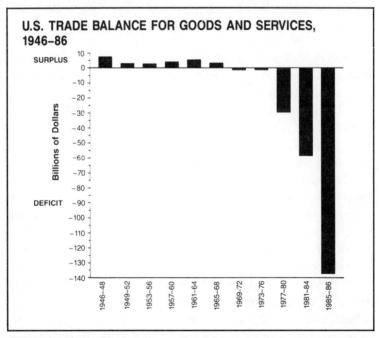

U.S. TRADE BALANCE FOR GOODS AND SERVICES, 1946–86

Figure 6: The United States experienced a small trade deficit for the first time in this century in 1971. In the 1980s, the deficit has escalated uncontrollably.

Source: *Economic Report of the President*, 1987, Table B-99.

money to invest that the United States was no longer their best choice for quick profits. The federal government's policies at this time encouraged U.S. multinationals and banks to participate actively in this expansion of investments outside the United States, rather than to plow profits back into the modernization of U.S. industrial capacity. In 1971, this situation created a U.S. balance of trade deficit for the first time since 1894.

Yet nothing was done to rebuild and modernize the American economy so we could compete more effectively in international trade. Political scientists John Zysman and Stephen Cohen's 1987 analysis of the range of actions that could and should have been taken highlights how little we recognized that the United States had exhausted the advantages it enjoyed at the end of World War II. Nothing was done to increase substantially the reinvestment of profits in the United States nor to improve the efficiency of production, marketing, and management techniques. Instead of a trade policy for modernization drawing effectively on all of the resources available to our government, only ad hoc band-aids were applied to America's emerging economic wounds. With investment slowing, more and more U.S. industries sought and received outright protection from foreign competition. The protection granted in the 1960s to various industries—including steel, dairy, and pianos, for example—was ineffective because the relief was not tied to specific commitments from those industries to modernize. Very few seized the opportunity, leaving the United States in an increasingly uncompetitive position. While the American family encountered a period of diminished opportunities and expectations, while household income stagnated, and while our national government failed to act decisively to retool, retrain, and rebuild America, the principal beneficiaries were those international bankers and multinational capitalists who were quite happy to move their money out of the United States to economies that promised more immediate and higher returns. Between 1971 and 1981, more than $480 billion was invested by U.S. corporations overseas rather than in America. This is almost two-thirds of the amount invested in the United States by all U.S. manufacturers for new plants and equipment during this period.

The Reagan Nonpolicy

The failure of industry to invest in America combined with the abdication of policy by the Reagan administration allowed the trade problem of the 1970s to blossom into a trade deficit of crisis proportions. Between 1981 and 1983, during the Reagan recession, the total value of our exports actually declined by more than 10 percent, led by a 15 percent decline in the real value of our merchandise exports. The following years showed more decreases than increases, and by 1986, the dollar value of our exports had not returned to the 1981 level. In real terms, exports were 5 percent less after five years of Reagan administration neglect than they were during the administration's first year. And while exports have been stagnating, our import bills have been skyrocketing. After a 3 percent drop in the real value of imports in 1982, imports have risen at a yearly average rate exceeding 10 percent. In sum, between 1981 and 1986, exports declined, in nominal terms, from $234 billion to $217 billion while imports rose from $273 billion to $387 billion. Hence, the trade deficit ballooned from $39 billion to $170 billion. Even as we were borrowing more and more heavily to pay for our imports, an additional $300 billion was taken out of the United States and invested in industries overseas. Only an administration blinded by the most rigid of ideologies could have failed to act in the face of these mounting threats to our future prospects.

Ultimately, the neglect of our manufacturing industries has led to a persistent and accelerating inability of the United States to pay its own way in the world economy. When the U.S. imports more than it can pay for with the earnings from its exports, it must either borrow funds from foreigners or finance its current consumption with income from past investments overseas. As a result, the United States has become the world's largest debtor nation, with an outstanding foreign debt of $260 billion, a staggering amount which swells with every passing month. Increasingly, we are also becoming a *rentier* nation, living off the coupons of previous overseas investments to pay for our imports rather than relying on the returns from our current exports of goods and services. In 1961, our exports of goods and services accounted for more than 80 percent of the cost of our imports; by 1986, exports paid only 55 percent of our import bill.

The Reagan approach was a nonpolicy, based on the shallow notion that free trade creates a wave of economic prosperity that reaches all shores. Yet of the roughly 12 million Americans who have lost their jobs in the manufacturing sectors of the U.S. economy since 1981, more than 3.75

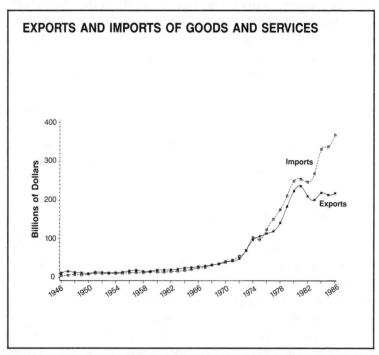

EXPORTS AND IMPORTS OF GOODS AND SERVICES

Figure 7: In the 1980s, imports have risen steadily while exports have stagnated. The resulting gap led to a massive trade deficit in 1986 of $170 billion.

Source: *Economic Report of the President*, 1987, Table B-99.

million were laid off as a direct result of competition from imports and our mounting trade deficits. These hard-working men and women, and the communities that depend on them, were thrown overboard by the Reagan administration, which was at the same time slashing the quality and the number of life rafts—unemployment insurance and job training programs—available to displaced workers.

Further, the rising tide of imports in the 1980s has accelerated and exacerbated the movement of the United States away from the production of goods and into the production of services, where fewer and fewer people are able to earn a decent living. Increasing market shares in almost every category of consumer and capital goods now consumed in the United States are held by foreign imports. For instance, up until 1978, virtually no electronic computing equipment was imported into the United States. In 1980, imports accounted for roughly 5 percent of domestic consumption, but by 1986, they accounted for more than 20 percent of all electronic computer purchases in the United States. In footwear, imports have risen from 17 percent of the market in 1972, to 32 percent in 1980, to more than 60 percent in 1986. And in the automobile industry, imports in 1986 accounted for 26 percent of U.S. purchases, compared with 8 percent in 1972 and 20 percent in 1980.

The Reagan administration simply abdicated responsibilty for the productive sectorrs of our economy, allowing them to be sacrificed to the myth of free trade. Much too late did the administration recognize the serious damage being done to American export and import-competing firms by the wildly overvalued dollar. The dollar appreciated in value by more than 45 percent between 1981 and 1985 due to Reagan's bizarre fiscal policies. This further helped to make U.S. exports uncompetitive in foreign markets while opening our market to a flood of imports. The annual interest payment on our foreign debt, now approaching $25 billion per year, is in part the surcharge on those imports that appeared so inexpensive due to the distortion in the exchange value of the dollar.

By 1986 it was clear that our trade deficit was out of control. Persistent trade deficits of more than $150 billion, more than three times the average deficit in 1979–81, brought forth deafening calls for action from Congress. Only then did the administration respond. Once it did acknowledge a problem, however, it acted in the mistaken belief that the damage could be reversed merely by bringing down the exchange value of the dollar. Unfortunately, plants that shut down when they cannot compete do not magically reopen when the dollar's value declines. While a stable dollar at a reasonable exchange rate is a necessary condition for American prosperity, it is not a sufficient condition. The American government must do more than close the barn door

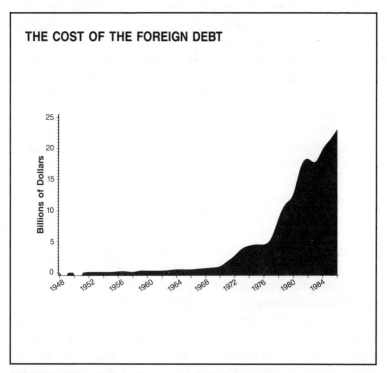

Figure 8: The interest on our foreign debt paid by the U.S. government to foreign individuals, banks, corporations, and governments has turned from a trickle into a flood.

Source: *Economic Report of the President*, 1987, Table B-19.

after the horse has already escaped.

Without greater productivity and enhanced competitiveness for our exporting industries, our ability to import goods from other countries depends on the willingness of foreign governments, along with foreign banks and investors, to finance our enormous current account deficits by continuing to acquire and hold increasingly devalued dollars. That willingness requires that our interest rates remain high. Our real interest rate—the nominal rate minus the inflation rate—stands 2 percent higher than that in Japan, for example. If we try to reduce our interest rates to encourage more investment in domestic industrial modernization, foreign investors will take their money and run. And they will do it quickly. More than $300 billion of the holdings of foreign governments, corporations, and banks are U.S. government securities, fully liquid at any time. More is in private securities also redeemable on short notice. Hence, within a few weeks or months of a substantial change in our relative interest rates, we could see a massive exodus of the capital that allows us to pay for our imports. We are hostage to international creditors until we rebuild the capacity to pay for our imports with our own exported products.

A prosperous world economy, based on thriving national economies and a robust exchange of goods and services, is critical to our national interest and that of our allies. Trade that builds upon our dynamic comparative advantage will enhance our own prosperity and that of a world economy dependent on us. Only with decisive action to reverse America's productive decline, to enable America to compete actively again in international markets, to make international trade once again the servant of our national interest and not its master, can we harness the power of international trade to the American economic engine. The Growth with Fairness program's international trade policies, detailed in this chapter, are designed to meet that goal.

An Effective International Trade Policy

Too many proposals made in recent years mistakenly adopt

a negative approach to solving our economic woes. Many have called for a broad program of tariff and quota protection, cutting off the United States from not only the costs, but also the benefits of international trade. Such proposals for protection fail to distinguish between American firms that are actively seeking to modernize and thus might be entitled to some temporary protection, and those inefficient firms that are seeking to hide from competition and thus would merely pass on the higher costs of their goods to American consumers.

Many people have called for targeted, punitive actions against specific trade partners, such as Japan, solely because they have accumulated substantial trade surpluses in their accounts with the United States. While proposals aimed at forcing our trade partners to behave reasonably and fairly in their export promotion and import restriction activities are eminently reasonable, there is no reason to assume that a trade surplus is, in and of itself, a symptom of unfair behavior. The U.S. trade surpluses from 1894 until 1971 were the result of high-quality, low-cost production of a wide range of agricultural, capital, and consumer goods. Proposals to bring balance back into our own trade account should not punish those who produce efficiently in the world and accumulate surpluses by adhering to the normal rules of play. We must focus instead on retaliating against the unfair trade practices that penalize our producers. At the same time, we must reverse those policies of our own government that encourage the export of jobs rather than of goods and services. Most importantly, we must focus our efforts on ensuring that our trade policy serves to encourage our own producers to become competitive at home and abroad, and thereby lay a solid foundation for sustainable growth.

Ultimately, we must recognize that the principal causes of our trade deficit lie in the actions of the U.S. government and America's producers, not in those of foreign firms or governments. Our trade policy should not only seek to persuade other countries to behave responsibly and fairly. It must also include vigorous actions, which we can take right here at home, to rebuild our competitiveness by once again making high-quality production at competitive costs the mark of American industry.

End Unfair Trade Practices by Foreign Governments

Not only by our words but also by our actions we must make it clear to our trading partners that unfair trading practices will no longer be tolerated. Those countries that take steps to give their producers unjust advantage over their American competitors must know that they will face swift and certain retaliation when they seek to sell in American markets. Two distinct kinds of practices by our trade partners must be addressed by any administration seriously committed to ensuring an international trading system that allows our firms to compete on just terms.

Existing regulations against product dumping, improper export subsidies, and discrimination against U.S. imports are insufficient. When a product is being marketed in the United States at a price lower than its production cost, or when a foreign government is restricting access by U.S. firms to its markets, retaliation is presently left to the discretion of the president. This discretion was used too often by the Reagan administration as an excuse for inaction. Paralyzed by the myth of a free market and the glorification of cutthroat competition, this administration ignored calls for remedial action in the face of overwhelming evidence of unfair trade practices.

The U.S. International Trade Commission is already charged with the task of investigating possible violations of fair trade practices. For example, in 1985, the ITC completed more than 250 investigations of alleged unfair trade practices under provisions of federal law originating in the Tariff Act of 1930, the Trade Act of 1974, the Trade Agreements Act of 1979, and the Agricultural Adjustment Act. The ITC has established a reputation as an objective and effective monitor of U.S. interests in assessing the practices of our trading partners. It is a nonpartisan body, with a membership mandated by law to consist of five commissioners—two Democrats, two

Republicans, and one Independent. It is a body that responds to requests from, and reports to, both the executive and the legislative branches of government. Its budget is submitted to the president; however, its request for funding must be passed on to Congress as received by the White House, without interference by the Office of Management and Budget. For these reasons, ITC funding, staff levels, and investigations have increased during the Reagan years, and the agency's integrity has remained intact. The ITC professional staff is widely credited with providing to the commission solid and balanced analyses, which the commission's recommendations normally follow closely. They merit the support and respect that thorough and impartial judgments of difficult and complex questions deserve.

The ITC findings of product dumping are only advisory to the president. As a result, President Reagan was free to ignore its findings of unfair trade practices. For example, in 1985, he ignored recommendations from the ITC that the footwear industry be granted emergency protection from unfair competition. According to one calculation, President Reagan and his predecessors responded negatively to ITC recommendations in fully two-thirds of all cases, refusing the protection requested or offering less protection than recommended.

Therefore, the first trade policy of this program for Growth with Fairness would give greater authority to the ITC and require that retaliatory tariffs be automatically imposed if the ITC so recommends in cases involving dumping, improper subsidies, or discrimination, unless negotiations between the United States and the offending country result in the end of the unfair trade practice within one year. By stiffening our resolve, we will send a clear message to foreign governments and producers that the United States is committed to trade that is free so long as that trade is fair. By mandating a period of negotiations after a finding that products are being unfairly marketed in the United States, we will provide an opportunity to resolve international conflicts through diplomatic channels. By mandating automatic tariffs if the negotiations are unsuccessful, we will provide American negotiators the leverage required to reach a satisfactory resolution.

In addition to these traditional practices of subsidizing exports, dumping goods into the American market, and discriminating against U.S. imports, there is another important unfair trade practice that requires action: the exploitation of low-wage labor in Third World countries. U.S. policy ought to be governed by the principle that low production costs that result primarily from exploitative labor practices do not constitute a legitimate expression of comparative advantage. They have nothing to do with greater efficiency of production, nor do they express the kinds of choices likely to be made by democratic societies. The lower costs that attract multinationals stem entirely from sweatshop conditions in

---

THE ATARI STORY: U.S. WORKERS BE DAMNED

Typical of the export of U.S. manufacturing jobs to low-wage countries is the recent experience of the Atari Corp., once the darling of Warner Communications. In the late 1970s and early 1980s, Atari was an investor's dream, putting video games in over 5 million American homes and controlling a 40 percent share of the home computer market. It supplied Warner with nearly half of the parent company's total revenues and 70 percent of its operating earnings. In 1983, however, the bottom suddenly fell out for Atari, the victim of incompetent management and its inability to match the technological progress of competitors. In an attempt to rescue the firm from financial disaster and to preempt the unionization of its factories, the firm simply closed its U.S. assembly operations and moved them to Taiwan and Hong Kong. No warning was given. 1,700 American workers were summarily dismissed. Even a resolution by the Alabama state legislature asking Atari and Warner to "reassess their loyalties," was completely disregarded. According to *Business Week*, of March 14, 1983, Atari's flight was "just one more symptom in a company deeply sickened by faltering management." The price of this management failure has been paid by the company's former American workers. Of course, the management problems were not solved by relocation. In July 1984, Warner sold the company for only $30 million, barely covering what was paid to acquire it eight years before. Atari, like other runaway companies who move their operations abroad, is completely free to import the products of low-wage labor back into the U.S. market.

countries that forbid or severely repress free trade unions and disregard International Labor Organization standards for the health and safety of workers.

Much of the profit made by multinational firms derives from their export of American jobs through the creation of subsidiaries or through outsourcing to low-wage countries. In Taiwan and Korea, for instance, manufacturing wages are less than 25 percent of the U.S. level. In Sri Lanka, they are less than 5 percent. Much of the shift of U.S. production overseas has little to do with encouraging sound economic development in the Third World. Instead, opportunities for improved domestic productivity and competitiveness have been sacrificed by our multinationals on the altar of immediate profitability that depends primarily on the exploitation of low-wage labor. Far from deferring to such unfair labor practices, the U.S. government has the duty to defend American industry, its workers, and its communities against them.

To combat this practice, the Growth with Fairness program proposes that the president be granted authority to impose tariffs on imports where the main difference in the cost of producing those goods in America rather than in a foreign country derives from excessive differences in wages. This authority must be available especially in situations in which the State Department has found that governmental repression—or governmental tolerance of private repression —has materially affected the wage levels involved. The ITC would be mandated to expand its analysis of industries to include comparative wage rates. If it finds that wages are substantially lower in a foreign country compared with the wages paid for the same work done in the United States, and if wages comprise a substantial part of the costs of production, the president would enter into negotiations with the country involved when there is evidence of repression affecting wage rates. Should those negotiations fail to produce significant change in the wages, the president would then be authorized to impose tariffs up to a level that would compensate for the difference in costs of production stemming from the difference in wage rates.

Imposing tariffs on low-wage exporters to American markets must be handled with great care. There is always a danger that possibilities for development for Third World countries will be held hostage to protectionist demands in the United States. However, the threat to America's basic economic security posed by the hemorrhaging of jobs from America to sweatshops overseas is so great that we cannot afford inaction. Recognizing the hazards inherent in this policy, the proposal made here would provide the president with the authority to impose tariffs rather than the mandate to do so.

These two steps are the absolute minimum that must be undertaken to bring fairness into our trading relations. Vigorous diplomacy can and should go beyond these actions. Efforts to initiate multilateral discussions for systematic reform of the GATT are clearly needed. Pressure on Germany and Japan to stimulate their domestic economies to increase the opportunities for our exports must be maintained. Stiffer international sanctions against predatory trade practices must be sought. Yet we must also recognize that our ability to influence the sovereign behavior of other states is necessarily limited. We must not fall into the trap of relying exclusively on those efforts that can succeed only if other nations comply with our wishes. We must also look to our own actions, to those policies and programs that we can control and whose effectiveness we can shape directly.

U.S. Policies To Encourage Export of Goods, Not Jobs

When we look to our own actions, the first thing we can and must do is reverse those policies of the U.S. government that subsidize U.S. investment abroad and encourage the export of American jobs instead of goods. We must insure that such policies, which might have been well-intentioned and effective at an earlier time, are modified or eliminated when they no longer serve our national interests. Three specific proposals are part of the plan for Growth with Fairness.

Two of these proposals would improve America's ability to promote exports. First, the United States must coordinate a much-expanded program of technical assistance for U.S. exporters. A wide array of agencies and offices—from the International Trade Administration of the Commerce Department, to the Office of the Special Trade Representative, to the desk officers of the State Department—attempts to provide information to firms interested in exporting. In 1982, the federal government, in an effort to encourage small and medium-size firms to enter the export market, allowed such firms to join together in Export Trading Companies (ETCs) exempt from antitrust prohibitions; however, very few were formed. Without aggressive and coordinated arrangements designed to bring this information to the eyes and ears of America's small and medium-size producers, the impact of these programs will fall far short of their potential.

Therefore, the program for Growth with Fairness calls for the creation of a lead agency for export promotion. It could be in an existing agency, such as the International Trade Administration, or a newly created Department of International Trade. This lead agency would undertake not only to coordinate the various programs in place, but also to vigorously encourage America's small and medium-size firms to develop export markets. Further, it ought to be empowered to assist industry groups in developing export research and marketing consortia, and to actively encourage the creation of ETCs in areas where U.S. firms have competitive export opportunities.

In addition, existing agencies that provide financial as well as technical assistance to American exporters do not target that assistance to promote job creation. The Export-Import Bank and the Overseas Private Investment Corporation are the principal U.S. authorities that give exporters access to capital at internationally competitive rates. A large portion of Ex-Im Bank assistance currently goes to multinational firms. Similarly, OPIC loan guarantees work principally for multinationals, many of which produce their goods, even those with a "MADE IN USA" label, with a wide assortment of imported parts. More than $40 billion of U.S. manufacturing imports presently consist of intracompany exchanges, in which the goods are produced overseas by a subsidiary of a U.S. multinational corporation. The Ex-Im Bank and the OPIC need to target their assistance better, aiming only at those corporations that will maintain or increase the number of American jobs.

Therefore, the Growth with Fairness program proposes that the technical and financial assistance of U.S. export promotion efforts should be restricted to those products of which more than 90 percent of total value is produced within the United States. For example, the Ex-Im Bank should not lend any funds for an export contract unless it receives persuasive evidence that more than 90 percent of the total value of the exported goods will be produced in the United States. The expanded export promotion efforts of a lead agency for international trade might allow the United States to begin to match the kind of concerted efforts that are undertaken by other countries in promoting their exports. By restricting access to technical and finacial assistance, we should be assured that the beneficiaries of American efforts to promote exports would be American workers, not those in Taiwan, Korea, or Brazil.

Finally, the trade policies of Growth with Fairness require a change in the tax laws. The federal tax code contains provisions that perversely encourage the export of American productivity and jobs, thus weakening our trade position and frustrating domestic growth. The most important such provision is that which excludes from taxation the profits earned by the wholly owned foreign subsidiaries of American multinational firms until those profits are repatriated back to the U.S. parent company. The deferral of federal tax liability on these overseas earnings continues indefinitely, as long as the money is reinvested in that or any other foreign subsidiary. This provision was valuable immediately after World War II, when U.S. policy was dedicated to the task of reconstructing devastated European economies. It lost its rationale as those reconstructed economies became our chief trade competitors. The tax deferral of foreign subsidiary profits means that there exist greater incentives for the multinational firm to invest and continually reinvest overseas rather than to expand production at home. The federal tax code is not even neutral regarding the location of investment. It actually discourages domestic repatriation of profits. The result is a loss of American jobs and manufacturing capacity.

Tax reformers have tried for years to repeal this provision. President Kennedy in 1962 and President Carter in 1978 placed repeal high upon their list of needed tax corrections, but their efforts were resisted successfully by U.S. international business interests. Given the size of the current trade deficit and the comparative disadvantages of American manufacturers, the time has finally come to end this absurd tax privilege. The cost is moderately small—about three quarters of a billion dollars annually—but the main purpose of repeal is not revenue generation. It is simply wrong for the government to favor with American taxpayer dollars the flight of investment and production overseas. It is also wrong for profits earned by a U.S. parent company to be taxed more heavily than those earned by that company's subsidiaries abroad. Our public policy should be used to build up the American capacity to export, and not to subsidize the foreign manufacture, by our own national firms, of goods that we then import.

Modernization Tariffs

These steps to retaliate against those who participate in world trade without regard for the rules of the game, and to eliminate programs and policies that encourage the export of manufacturing jobs and discourage investment in the United States, are essential components of the Growth with Fairness strategy for a lasting economic recovery. However, negative actions alone are not enough. It is not in the American tradition to blame foreigners for problems that we, by positive steps, can solve. We must affirm that American producers and workers have a future in the world economy, that we can again compete successfully in a wide range of goods. To do so, we must attend to the immediate needs of American industry during its period of rebuilding. We must allow American firms to recover from years of neglect by investors and the government, and to modernize their products and their production processes so we can once again become a leader in the world economy. We must use our international trade policy not just to stem the tide of international imbalance, but also, and more importantly, to stimulate sustainable growth.

Therefore, the centerpiece of the Growth with Fairness policies proposed here is the use of "modernization tariffs" to be made available to the producers of manufactured goods that are critical to the industrial renewal of America. These industries would be given preferential access to domestic markets for a limited time period. The criteria for industries to receive this assistance would be identical to those for industries seeking financing from the Industrial Development Bank, namely 1) their job-creating potential, 2) their technological edge in world markets in both product and production process, and 3) the requirements of national defense and economic security. These tariffs would be limited in duration and in scope. They would be made available only to domestic producers who file with the ITC acceptable plans for modernizing their facilities, for expanding jobs, and for developing and serving international as well as domestic markets. The tariffs would apply for only five years and would not ordinarily be renewable.

American industries need breathing space to rebuild, retool, and retrain. This breathing space, provided by the modernization tariffs, would allow America to capitalize on its emerging comparative advantage in the production of goods that embody advanced technologies, either in the product or in the production process. We must recognize that only the short-sighted believe that comparative advantage is best served by asking at any moment what we could sell abroad. While instantaneous sales may appeal to those who evaluate the performance of a company solely by looking at the quarterly bottom line, any investor and any government attending to the national interest knows that the true measure of economic success lies in investing for the future. If that were not true, the Japanese would not be producing automobiles today, and the Koreans would not be producing steel. Certainly, in the 1950s and 1960s, respectively, neither of those countries had a comparative advantage with respect to the United States in those products. Nonetheless, by looking to the future and investing heavily in that future, those countries have demonstrated what we must do.

In steel and motorcycles, the Reagan administration was dragged into arrangements of this sort. In the motorcycle industry, for example, the results already have been very favorable. In 1983, Harley-Davidson Corporation advised the Reagan administration that foreign competitors, particularly Kawasaki, were making it impossible for Harley to continue producing high-powered motorcycles with engines larger than 700 ccs. They made it plain that what they sought was temporary relief and that they had in mind a specific modernization plan which, once completed, would allow them to compete successfully in free and fair markets. They asked for five years of protection and the administration grudgingly acceded. Less than four years later, in March 1987, Harley-Davidson's management announced that the modernization program had proceeded so smoothly that they no longer required protection. They even requested that the tariffs be removed.

The successful rebuilding of the motorcycle industry was, to a certain extent, serendipitous. The tariff relief granted by the president to Harley-Davidson did not incorporate any binding commitment to modernize. Had Harley chosen to use the period of protection merely to amass profits behind a wall of protection, no legal action could have been taken against it. The consequences of a failure to mandate modernization as a condition of receiving the tariff assistance can be seen most clearly in the recent experience of the steel industry.

In steel, the benefits of protection were not tied explicitly to plans for industrial regeneration. Yet, in his "Steel Import Relief Determination" of 1984, President Reagan made it clear that a wide range of tools, including tariffs when necessary, would be used to try to restrict steel imports, excluding semifinished steel, to "a more normal level" of 18.5 percent of domestic purchases. At the time, that ratio was 26.5 percent, up from 14.2 percent in 1976. While some investment has taken place in the steel industry during this period of protection, much of the profit from that protection was used by the steel companies to diversify out of steel products or to merge rather than to rebuild. The management of U.S. Steel alone has spent more than $10 billion since 1981 to acquire nonsteel-related subsidiaries, and it has indicated the depth of its commitment to the future of steel production facilities by changing the corporate name in July 1986 to USX.

The proposal for short-run tariff assistance presumes that the benefits of protection must only be given to firms in industries that have committed themselves to modernization. Those commitments should be legally enforceable, not accepted as matters of faith. The goal is not to insulate our firms from international markets but to help them, quickly and decisively, to enter those markets. An administration that cares about the well-being of its working population and that seeks to encourage a pattern of sustained and sustainable growth should proceed voluntarily and vigorously, not dragging and kicking, to take those actions that will allow our critical manufacturing industries to rebuild. America's workers, both employed and unemployed, should once again have a government that is eager to act on their behalf, rather than one that clings tenaciously to outdated theories and ideological tenets that leave America's industries and workers vulnerable in a highly interdependent world economy.

We should not pretend, however, that every firm and every industry can or should be rescued from international competition. While we all will benefit in the long run from a free and fair world trading system, we must accept the responsibility to assist those who pay in the present for our collective long-term benefit. This program for Growth with Fairness calls for every worker who loses his or her job as a result of international competition to be guaranteed a place in a state-administered or -regulated job training and placement program. Assistance of this kind was available, although not guaranteed, under the Trade Assistance Adjustment Act. When the programs under that act were replaced during the Reagan administration by the Job Training Partnership Act, those workers displaced by foreign trade were tossed into the pool of all those needing job training assistance. While some help is presently available under the JTPA, we must extend and enhance coverage to all workers displaced by foreign competition. This is best handled as a part of a renewed federal and state commitment to effective job training programs, as discussed in chapter 4.

Modernization tariffs tied to explicit commitments to reinvest in plants and equipment, combined with comprehensive, accessible, and effective training programs for displaced workers, make up the essential core of an effective and forward-looking international trade policy. With these tariffs in our federal government's repertory, we shall no longer have to endure the embarrassment of our government's passivity in the face of international challenges to our future prosperity. We shall no longer be forced to take solely defensive actions, knowing that firms and industries might sit comfortably behind a protective curtain reaping short-term profits without taking the opportunity to build for the future. With a national training program in place, we could rest secure in the knowledge that workers in industries that, even with modernization, would be unable to compete will be cared for and brought back into the productive mainstream with a minimum of delay. With these tariffs in hand, we could expect our government to insist on binding commitments that modernization will take place before an industry gets any protection from international competition. If the effort to retool, retrain, and rebuild is undertaken, the federal government will have, with these modernization tariffs, appropriate instruments with which to nurture our national return to international competitiveness.

Conclusion

The overvalued U.S. dollar at long last has been corrected. Nonetheless, our trade deficit remains fixed at a level higher than at any time in our history. More positive policies are required if we are to reduce the trade deficit significantly. The United States needs vigorous trade measures that directly serve our national goal of industrial renewal. A three-pronged policy has been laid out in this chapter. It calls for 1) aggressive measures by the United States to terminate the dumping of foreign products in U.S. markets, to eliminate the competitive advantages in U.S. markets of products made by sweatshop labor, and to retaliate against discrimination aimed at U.S. exports; 2) the reversal of U.S. tax and other incentives that encourage multinational firms to transfer production out of the United States; and 3) selective modernization tariffs to protect for limited periods of time the U.S. market for firms that demonstrate the clear intention to modernize their products and production processes so that they can become, or remain, competitive in world markets. This last measure complements the industrial development policy outlined in chapter 2 and follows the very successful precedent established by Japan after World War II.

While focusing on these three areas of new initiatives designed to harness once again the power of international trade to the carriage of American growth with fairness, it will also be necessary to undertake a series of actions at the international level. We must take vigorous steps to strengthen international sanctions against nations that pursue predatory trade practices to gain an unfair advantage in U.S. markets. We must initiate a new round of GATT negotiations to devise a more sensible set of multilateral rules to govern a world in which trade in services is largely unregulated and in which much international trade involves intracompany multinational corporate transactions. We must move to relieve the Third World debt crisis by insisting that U.S. banks write down a certain portion of their excessive loans to Third World countries and accept those losses as the consequences of their own imprudent business judgments in the past. Unless these steps are taken, the world trading system will continue to limp along from crisis to crisis, much as it has for the last decade or more.

These international steps joined to the three areas of unilateral domestic initiatives just presented would help the U.S. economy in a manner consistent with our full participation in the growth and development of an integrated world economy. In an international trading system that is fair and free, America would again be prepared to take on the competition, both at home and abroad. Through such positive measures that avoid the extremes of mindless protectionism and mindless free trade, we can bring our massive trade deficit under control.

Chapter 4:

SOCIAL AND HUMAN RESOURCES POLICY

Since the beginning of the twentieth century, and especially since World War II, all advanced industrial countries have adopted measures aimed at improving the economic productivity of their citizens and underwriting human needs. They have worked to improve the quality of life at the workplace and in communities; to eliminate invidious discrimination because of age, sex, race, and ethnic origin; and to provide minimum levels of assistance to the aged, disabled, and destitute. The historic American tradition always has been one of concern for one's fellow citizens, of a community of individuals founded upon mutual respect and neighborly assistance in times of need. Gradually, we reached bipartisan understanding that government has a necessary role to play in the progress of a just society, both in the policies it implements and in the attitudes it fosters. Despite our differences, we all understand that economic security and economic dynamism are mutually reinforcing, that growth and fairness go together.

It was Franklin Roosevelt who first declared, in his 1944 State of the Union address, that we must guarantee to our citizens economic rights as firmly entrenched as the political and social rights we already enjoy. We cannot measure a nation's well-being by relying only on aggregate statistics such as the gross national product or the balance of trade. The ultimate goal of our productive efforts is not statistical superiority, but more extensive individual health and happiness. Aggregate wholes depend on the sum of their parts. An arithmetical growthmanship that is blind to its human foundations both sanctions the most grievous inequalities and injustices, and risks undermining that very growthmanship by neglecting to develop the capacities of its work force.

We must declare it self-evident, as did Roosevelt, that every American should have a right to a useful job; to earn enough to provide for his or her family; to have a decent home, adequate medical care, and a good education; and to be protected from the economic fears that accompany aging, illness, dependency, and unemployment. These are national goals critical to a society worthy of pride at home and admiration from abroad. Yet in recent years this seems to have been forgotten. The Reagan administration, with its language of acquisitive, self-centered individualism, told us that it is acceptable to neglect the community and disregard our collective responsibilities. The administration made it more difficult than before for the average family to win economic security. It even refused to acknowledge the fact of extensive hunger and homelessness in this land of abundance or to concede that government has an obligation to aid the victims. Fortunately, the tide of public opinion has begun to turn. The American people are becoming increasingly aware of the social and economic costs of the Reagan approach. But ending Reagan's policies alone will not be sufficient. We need positive and innovative steps to ensure the continued march of growth with fairness.

Holes in the Safety Net

After years of Reagan administration slashing, the American "safety net" is torn and tattered. The poor have suffered disproportionately from Reagan's budget cuts. Federal spending for Aid to Dependent Children through FY 1984 was 14.3 percent lower than projected from the pre-Reagan baseline, calculated from the rules and regulations in effect before Reagan administration changes. Food stamp outlays were 13.8 percent lower, unemployment insurance 17.4 percent lower, and child nutrition outlays 28 percent lower. Moreover, in each case, the cuts enacted by Congress were dramatically less than had been requested by the administration. The Reagan attack has restricted eligibility for social welfare programs so that fewer poor families qualify for federal assistance. It has also reduced program standards for families receiving aid, lowering the probability that they will attain a subsistence income.

In addition to stinginess with finances, the administration has promoted a meanness of spirit. We have been told that ketchup is a vegetable suitable for school lunches, that the homeless choose to sleep in the streets, that welfare payments are squandered on vodka, that the elderly make excessive use of their medical care, and that welfare is a principal cause of poverty. The implication is that we need not look beyond the pursuit of our own affluence, that the skewed distribution of income exists for some economically sound reason, that the victims are responsible for their own plight, and that we can thus callously disregard the misfortunes of others.

The net result, not unexpectedly, has been a sizable increase in poverty in America. The fundamental cause is a stagnating economy and the growing failure of the safety net to assist those in need of support. According to U.S. Census Bureau data, more than 31 million Americans have been poor during each of the Reagan years, by far the highest level since the War on Poverty was first launched and at least 5 million more than were poor in 1979. In every year under Reagan, between 13.6 and 15.2 percent of the total U.S. population

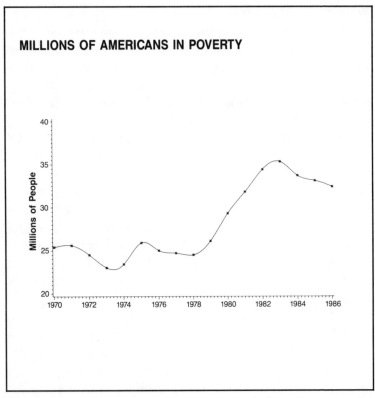

Figure 9: The number of Americans living in poverty, after accounting for cash payments from the government, is significantly higher in the 1980s than it has been for more than 15 years.

Source: U.S. Department of Commerce, Bureau of the Census, Current Population Reports, Series P-60, no. 157, *Money Income and Poverty: Status of Families and Persons in the United States*, 1986 (issued July 1987), Table 16.

has been officially counted as poor, in contrast with a yearly average of 11.8 percent during the 1970s. More than a third of all female-headed households are poor. More than a third of all minority households are poor. About a third of all children will spend at least a year in a poverty household by their 15th birthday. It also should be noted that the official U.S. definition of poverty already takes into account the effects of government cash transfer payments, including Social Security. Approximately one in four Americans falls below the designated standard prior to government intervention. Surely this is appalling for a country as rich as ours.

Statistics on who is poor reveal two important facts. First, poverty in most households is a temporary problem. According to data from the Panel Study on Income Dynamics, only one-twelfth of the Americans experiencing poverty between 1969 and 1978 remained poor for 8 or more of those 10 years. For a majority, poverty lasted merely 1 or 2 years. Its occurrence was not a function of a distinct and pernicious "culture of poverty," but was brought about by special and often tragic circumstances—illness, desertion, pregnancy, unemployment—that interfered with a family's ability to earn a suitable income. Second, many poor people already work. Approximately 40 percent of poor individuals older than 15 work full or part time; the overwhelming proportion of those who do not work are either single mothers with young children or individuals who are disabled, retired, or going to school. But employment does not necessarily yield enough income to deliver one from destitution. Of the entire U.S. population older than 15, nearly 4 percent—or 7.5 million people—worked full time in 1985 but did not earn enough by the U.S. Census Bureau count to escape poverty.

It is wrong to assume that the poor, by their lack of current success, do not fully aspire to the American dream. We must break away from the attitude of extreme suspicion and distrust promulgated by the Reagan administration. We must ensure jobs at reasonable wages and provide training so that people may take advantage of them. We must help those seeking to escape the scourge of poverty to build a self-reliant future. To those who remain unable to maintain subsistence for themselves and their families, we must willingly provide assistance on decent and dignified terms. Too many among us have once been poor, or can envision becoming poor, for us to adopt a different position.

The present American welfare system does not adequately achieve these ends. It is composed of a myriad of programs with little coordination and inconsistent coverage. Various in-kind benefits, for example, are earmarked for specific kinds of goods. Cash benefits are of two sorts: insurance programs financed by the recipients themselves through their payroll taxes, and means-tested programs financed out of general revenues in which eligibility is restricted to specific categories, such as the needy elderly, blind, and disabled, and to female-headed or, in some cases, unemployed families with dependent children. The categorical nature of the American welfare system is important for it accords very different treatment to different groups of equally needy individuals. According to data from Daniel Weinberg, an economist with the U.S. Department of Health and Human Services, more than 99 percent of the elderly poor in 1984 received government cash and in-kind benefits, which filled 98 percent of the gap between their market income and the poverty threshold. By contrast, 86 percent of single-parent poor households received government benefits, and the amounts were much less generous, lifting only about 40 percent above poverty.

Most tragic of all, many poor households, those that do *not* fall within the specified categories, receive not a cent in cash assistance from the federal government. These include single non-elderly individuals and married couples without children. They also include many stable, two-parent families with children, especially the working poor. To be sure, such families can receive certain in-kind aid such as food stamps, and some states have general assistance programs although they tend to be small. But according to Weinberg, only 59 percent of the poor two-parent families with children obtained any kind of government welfare in 1984, and the amounts brought only one-quarter of them out of poverty. In general, the able-bodied and working poor have been left coldheartedly to fend for themselves. As a society, we seem to lose our compassion at the doorway to the private market.

The American War on Poverty, which Lyndon Johnson declared in 1965, has for the last few years been in retreat. The United States has dropped behind comparable industrial societies in its efforts to reduce the poverty rate and to bring its citizens back into the economic mainstream. It is urgent that we resume that effort. We must prevent reversal of the victories won in the battle for the elderly. We must redouble our efforts to assist the current welfare population and to help it become self-supporting. We must open a new front to aid those families struggling to survive in a precarious marketplace. Most important, we must regain our sense of commitment and caring about the fate of others. Anything less means defeat.

The restoration of vigorous economic growth will contribute much. The poor and disadvantaged fare better in a buoyant economy. To be meaningful, however, that growth must be channeled in directions that expand the available quantity of decently paying jobs, and it must be supplemented by government programs that enable more individuals to make the most of their opportunities. Only then can we effectively lower the number of our citizens whose well-being depends upon our generosity. Growth without fairness is empty. It is also self-defeating. We cannot continue to grow without a better educated and more skilled work force.

A meaningful policy for social and human resources, intended to advance the health and welfare of all individuals, is composed of three essential parts. It must provide direct assistance to those deserving households whose income falls below acceptable standards. It must help disadvantaged, displaced, and low-income workers better develop their skills and adapt to technological changes, both for their own self-esteem and for our national economic future. And it must guarantee that every worker is given the full protection of the law, is respected in the workplace, and is able to live in a safe and stable community. America has made great progress in the decades since the end of World War II in instituting the kind of social and human resources policy our citizens require. We have, for example, expanded Social Security, introduced Head Start and the Jobs Corps, and established regulations for equal employment opportunity and occupational safety. But while Americans can be pleased with these achievements, we nevertheless should not rest content. There is more to be done to ensure social justice and extend the opportunities of full participation to all.

The program for Growth with Fairness proposes new in-itiatives in each of these three essential areas of social and human resources policy: 1) a long-overdue reform of the wel-fare system, as advocated vigorously for many years by our state governors and by the National Conference of Catholic Bishops, in which the federal government would assume financial responsibility for an acceptable level of payments to the needy, standardize benefits to guarantee equal treat-ment to all recipients, and revise the provisions affecting work incentives and protection of family units; 2) a new federal compact with the states in which the federal government, by taking the financial responsibility for the national health and welfare safety net, would absorb $27 billion in costs cur-rently borne by the states, and the states in turn would be required to use the money thereby saved for programs both to improve the quality and availability of education, job train-ing, child care, and other social services and to promote job-creating economic development; and 3) a series of vigorous actions undertaken by the federal government to protect the economic rights of all its citizens, including protections against discrimination, inhuman work conditions, and ar-bitrary plant closings. Fairness is not a matter for the poor and disadvantaged alone. It affects the lives of every one of us and is fundamental to our vision of a prosperous society.

National Welfare Reform

The key word in this proposal for national welfare reform is *national*. Among cash transfer programs, Social Security has always been run by the federal government, with financ-ing, eligibility, and payment levels set at the national level. It is a universal and uniform program, encompassing all Americans equally and treating all recipients according to the same rules and regulations. Supplemental Security Income for the indigent aged, blind, and disabled has been a feder-ally run program since it was reformed in 1972. Aid to Families with Dependent Children, however, is a mixed ven-ture. The individual states have always had primary responsibility for defining eligibility and allowable benefits, while the federal government merely provides about 54 percent of the funds and establishes broad guidelines. AFDC, therefore, is really a label for 50 radically different programs, resulting in widely unequal treatment for equally deserving Americans depending on where they live. Similarly, among in-kind benefit programs, food stamps is a federal program, administered by the U.S. Department of Agriculture. Medicare, the health insurance program for the elderly, is considered part of the Social Security structure and thus is also completely national. Medicaid, however, which is noninsured health care for the needy, is, like AFDC, a mixed venture. The states determine most of the regulations, the federal government supplies most of the funds, and the result is widely uneven treatment of equally destitute individuals.

The Growth with Fairness program calls for the federal government to assume the financial and program responsibilities for AFDC and Medicaid, ending the joint partnership as it previously did with SSI. In FY 1986, total AFDC outlays totaled approximately $16 billion; total Medicaid outlays were nearly $45 billion. The state share of these two programs was approximately $27 billion. Under the reform proposed here, this cost would be assumed by the federal government, adding to budgeted expenditures but producing equivalent savings to the states. These savings would provide a substantial dollar basis for a new federal compact, to be described below.

Shifting responsibility for AFDC to the national level would do far more than readjust financial burdens. It would also achieve more fair treatment, ending offensive interstate disparities. States, for example, differ in the kind of agency that administers AFDC, in the speed with which they must process applications, in the information they require of applicants and recipients, in the conditions for hearings and appeals, and in the definition of the assistance family unit and of what constitutes a suitable home for dependent children. Most important are the interstate differences in payment levels. The states now differ widely in their definitions of the maximum permissible AFDC award and in the payments actually made. The mean payment per AFDC family in the five most generous states in 1985 averaged $500, more than three-and-a-half times the mean payment, averaging $135, in the five least generous states. The mean payment in Alaska, for example, was $550 per family, and in California it was $514. By contrast, the mean family payment in Mississippi was only $104, and in Alabama it was $113.

As we are one nation, there is no justifiable reason for such extreme differences. It constitutes, in essence, abject discrimination on the basis of residence. National welfare reform would eliminate unfair divergences in state administrative practices and eligibility rules, establishing much more uniform treatment under the law. It would equalize payment rates to equally needy AFDC recipients. It would also introduce three necessary changes in the law.

First, we must guarantee that the family without income obtains an acceptable cash benefit. This would be done under the Growth with Fairness program by making the federal government entirely responsible for all AFDC benefits up to a maximum payment level set at 55 percent of the U.S. poverty threshold. For a family of four with no countable income in 1985, for example, the federal maximum guarantee would have been $504 per month. Food stamps would have given that family another $264 worth of income, and Medicaid on average would have given another $143, bringing the family virtually up to the minimum poverty threshold.

The $504 monthly federal AFDC guarantee in 1985 would have been greater than the prevailing level in 39 of the states as well as in the District of Columbia, Guam, Puerto Rico, and the Virgin Islands. Recipients in all these states and territories would have experienced a net gain in benefits. However, in 11 states the federal guarantee would have been lower than that already in place. To maintain benefit levels, those states will be requested to supplement federal AFDC payments out of their own revenues. This is how the reformed SSI operates, and the AFDC program structure proposed here is similar. It should be noted that the savings to

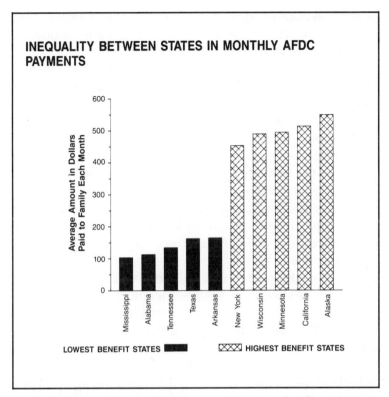

INEQUALITY BETWEEN STATES IN MONTHLY AFDC PAYMENTS

Average Amount in Dollars Paid to Family Each Month

LOWEST BENEFIT STATES ■■■■   ⊠⊠⊠ HIGHEST BENEFIT STATES

Figure 10: There exists a great disparity among states' welfare payments to families with dependent children. As a result, equally needy families now receive widely unequal treatment.

Source: *Social Security Bulletin, Annual Statistical Supplement*, 1987, Table 205.

the states resulting from the federal government's assumption of AFDC costs, up to 55 percent of the poverty standard, would provide those states that choose to supplement the payments more than ample funds to do so. Full supplementation up to existing payment levels would absorb only a third of the proposed savings to these 11 states. No state would be made worse off by the reform.

A further adjustment would also tend to help the more generous states. The cost of living varies widely across regions, yet this is not reflected in the official computation of the poverty rate. A $504 monthly grant will purchase a larger basket of goods and services in South Carolina than in New York. This is unfair. Therefore, the national poverty threshold should be adjusted for differences in living costs, and this adjusted threshold should then be used to calculate maximum federal AFDC payments. The additional burden to the federal budget for nationalizing AFDC up to 55 percent of the current poverty level and adjusting for the cost of living would be about $3 billion annually.

Second, it is necessary to restore to the welfare system the incentive for individuals to earn their way out of poverty. Americans have always believed in self-reliance, and attitudinal surveys show that the poor themselves overwhelmingly agree. Employment is not always a feasible substitute for relief, yet welfare rules must be structured to make it rational for every recipient to want to earn as much as possible. Perversely, the Reagan administration sought exactly the opposite. For all the outcry about ending dependency, it cut nominal program costs by making it less attractive for the AFDC adult to work. The effect has been to give many poor families the cruel choice between losing benefits or stopping work. This is a shortsighted approach that only hurts those wishing to help themselves. The system of "thirty and a third" had permitted welfare recipients who worked to disregard, when computing eligibility, the first $30 of earned monthly income and one-third of the amount above that. The Reagan administration requested that this work incentive operate for just the initial four months of payments, and thereafter benefits would be reduced dollar-for-dollar—in essence, a 100 percent tax on earnings. In place of "thirty and a third," the administration proposed mandatory state workfare programs for AFDC mothers unless their children were younger than three. Although Congress refused to allow the most extreme administration requests, the resulting compromise did give the welfare mother much less incentive to seek employment than before. It also restricted child care expenses for full-time workers to $160 per month and capped other work expense deductions at $75 per month.

The Reagan administration called itself a defender of the

free market and of the ability of individuals to rationally choose the best course, given marketplace incentives and disincentives. It proclaimed itself an opponent of heavy-handed government regulation and of blatant coercion. In the area of work and welfare, however, it clearly contradicted its own announced principles. The Growth with Fairness plan would restore the system of "thirty and a third" and expand deductions for work-related and child care expenses. The estimated cost would be approximately $500 million annually. This is a small price for writing back into the rules governing welfare the motivation for AFDC recipients to earn the most they possibly can for themselves and their families. It is a small price to pay for restoring dignity to the earning poor. It is a small price to pay for declaring that dependency should not be viewed as a permanent condition.

Third, the needs of poor two-parent families who are not presently entitled to federal cash assistance must be met. It is unjust discrimination when equally poor children are treated differently by the government—receiving different levels of food, shelter, medical care, and the other necessities of life—simply because of the number of adults in their family. In fact, the incentive is for the father to leave home. Often, if he deserts his loved ones, they can qualify for AFDC, Medicaid, and emergency benefits. If he stays, they must subsist on his meager wages, possibly supplemented by food stamps. With true irony, the current American welfare system functions to destroy the foundations of the secure family striving to maintain itself despite economic adversity.

Ideally, the United States should institute some form of guaranteed income that would grant benefits to all deserving poor individuals and households, whether with dependent children or not, as long as it included an enforceable work requirement for those able to work. President Nixon proposed a scheme of this sort, which passed the House in 1970 but did not emerge from Senate committee. A guaranteed income program, however, faces a difficult political dilemma. If payment levels are set too low, current welfare recipients will lose benefits. If they are set too high, the total cost will appear prohibitive and will unleash fears about work disincentives. Short of a guaranteed income for all, the federal government could open the AFDC program, with its payment limits and strict eligibility rules, to every needy household that contains young dependent children. Such a policy would declare that, at a minimum, the children of this nation will receive sufficient assistance, regardless of family composition or circumstances. It would be a wise investment in America's future, in the citizens and productive workers of the next generation. The dollar cost of a greatly expanded AFDC, however, would still be significant, especially given the current budget situation.

There is, however, one change that can and should be adopted immediately. The states presently have the option of instituting an AFDC-UP program, which permits payment to those two-parent households in which the prime earner is involuntarily unemployed or underemployed and which meet all the other, quite stringent AFDC criteria. The AFDC-UP program should become mandatory. It was started as an experimental program during the Kennedy administration and has remained relatively small. Twenty-four states, along with Guam and the District of Columbia, have introduced such a program; 26 states, along with Puerto Rico and the Virgin Islands, have not. Assuming that family participation in the non-AFDC-UP states would occur in approximately the same proportion as in those with AFDC-UP, uniform application would increase the total welfare caseload by less than 3 percent. The approximate cost, even given our proposed reforms in payment levels, would be less than $500 million per year. It would be tragic if, for so slight an addition to net federal welfare outlays, we failed to undertake this important first step in the direction of family preservation and child support.

Turning to health protection, the state rules governing Medicaid are even more complex and more inegalitarian than those for AFDC. First, Medicaid is optional for the states. Arizona has never adopted a Medicaid plan although it now does run a small, experimental demonstration project. Second, Medicaid recipients are divided into two broad classes of eligibility: categorically and medically needy. The categorically eligible include all recipients of AFDC and SSI, except in those 14 states that had more restrictive criteria before the 1972 federal assumption of SSI. It is not necessary for states to cover the medically needy classification, and 19 do not. All states that do, however, must give benefits to children in poor households and have the option of including the parents of those children, the blind, the elderly, and the disabled. Third, states vary in their administrative practices for application and physician reimbursement, as well as in the medical services offered.

Approximately 70 percent of Medicaid recipients are dependent children and their families, yet this group absorbs only one-quarter of total Medicaid costs. Approximately one-quarter of Medicaid recipients are aged, blind, or disabled, yet because of their greater medical needs this group absorbs more than 70 percent of total costs. Although Medicaid assists more than 22 million persons annually, it fails, according to a Congressional Budget Office study, to reach roughly half of all Americans with incomes below the poverty threshold. These are primarily poor, non-elderly single individuals and childless couples to whom the federal government denies Medicaid, and those potentially eligible recipients who live in states with restrictive income criteria or without the appropriate optional coverages.

The Growth with Fairness program calls for the federal government to assume all Medicaid costs, and it calls for program standardization to correct for much of the current unfairness. It proposes that Medicaid cover a wide range of important medical services to be provided for all individuals receiving or eligible for AFDC and SSI, and for all the elderly, blind, disabled, and dependent children deemed medically needy. The states would then have the discretion to provide expanded or supplemental coverage out of their savings. The federal government would establish reasonable regulations for reimbursement and procedures for administration, helping to control the now rampant inflation in medical costs. The goal of Medicaid reform is to improve health service rationing with better cost containment. It will promote more equal treatment for needy Americans and help more of them gain access to health care services. The net cost of standardization to the federal budget will be approximately $5 billion extra per year. This will bring the annual increase in the total price for all federal health and welfare programs proposed here to $35 billion, $27 billion of which represent savings to the states.

Failure to guarantee decent health care for all citizens is a tragedy to those who cannot afford necessary treatment. It is a loss to the nation of potentially productive human beings. It symbolizes the misplaced priorities in our public policies. Yet the reforms suggested here are only partial. America will never have justice in the area of health care until all persons are covered by some form of medical and hospital insurance. Most urgent is the need to extend government assistance to the working poor, including those whose incomes may reach above the poverty line but whose jobs carry no provision for health care and whose salaries do not afford adequate private insurance. However, as crucial as health care policy is, significant new initiatives will prove very costly. In this period of scarce budget resources, we must be content with less than ideal options. The federal government should therefore explore with private business ways to give health protection to the nation's work force. For example, employers should be required to provide adequate hospital and health insurance for all their employees. The government can help by establishing pooling arrangements that reduce the costs and lower the risks for small and medium-size firms.

The proposals of Growth with Fairness are designed to reduce the number of our fallen and the extent of their misfortune. Nevertheless, some will fall. It is of the utmost importance to decide how we shall treat them. Any system of poverty relief that castigates the poor for their lack of market success, that views misfortune as an individual's own problem, and that places aid to the needy lowest among all budget priorities fails by the historic standards of our own society. Justice must be the first principle of welfare reform.

The American tradition teaches us never to harden our hearts against suffering. We must treat all poor individuals as full members of our community, and we must address their unfulfilled needs with compassion.

To an extent, this requires money. The Growth with Fairness programs outlined above recommend that the federal government spend approximately $35 billion more than it does at present on individual health and welfare. This money is intended to mitigate the distress caused by deficient market income. Yet it is also the American way to lessen the probability that market incomes will be insufficient. We do not wish to leave those persons capable of making a productive contribution to society dependent upon government. Every American should be helped to fulfill his or her potential and to flourish independently in an expanding marketplace. Under the new federal compact proposed in this book, this is a task to be performed primarily by the states.

A New Federal Compact

The character of the federal partnership between the national and state governments is a dynamic one, evolving as the country grows and develops. In each era, the balance between autonomy and cooperation has been adapted to changing conditions and policy demands. We have reached a new stage in that continuing evolution. The time has come for a new federal compact, in which the states and the central government explicitly agree to shift certain domestic policy duties and financial obligations.

The Reagan administration talked much about federalism, but a federalism of the wrong and ineffectual sort. It sought to reverse the twentieth-century pattern of cooperative partnership and to reinstate instead the historically antiquated idea of segmented and separate domains. It spoke the language of improving state and local policy capability but instead stringently cut back on essential fiscal assistance. Between FY 1981 and 1986, grants-in-aid were slashed from 8.5 percent of total federal outlays to 6.1 percent. Had the percentage remained constant, the states and localities would have received $26.3 billion more in financial support.

Federalism without funding is a fraud. The idea was used under Reagan as a mere pretext for dismantling domestic social programs. Obligations would be given over to the states without the resources to perform them. The states would be left with the choice of curtailing benefits or raising taxes. The only responsibilities effectively delegated to the states would be to administer the reductions and to impose the sacrifices. Thus, the states would be trapped into complicity with Reagan's attack on government.

Nowhere is this clearer than in human resources policy. On the one hand, the Reagan administration proposed that the many special and categorical grants be consolidated into larger block grants. The block grants imposed fewer regulatory requirements from Washington, simplifying the system of intergovernmental monetary flows and permitting more state discretion and administrative flexibility in pursuing program objectives. On the other hand, the administration attached to each grant proposal a substantially reduced request for funding. Budget authority under education assistance grants, for example—including programs for improving reading, mathematics, and writing in the nation's primary schools; for training teachers; and for upgrading school facilities— was reduced by 30 percent from the pre-Reagan baseline over three years. Social services grants—covering day care, legal services, institutional care, programs to prevent or remedy child abuse or neglect, and programs to foster economic self-support—were cut by nearly 25 percent per year. Community services grants—those intended to provide locally based services to aid low-income individuals—lost more than 37 percent of their funds. Altogether, federal outlays in the budget category titled "Education, Training, Employment and Social Services" declined between FY 1981 and 1986 from 5.0 percent to 3.1 percent of total spending, the equivalent of an $18.9 billion reduction.

A true federalism should recognize that the different levels of government are intricately bound together and that effective policy implementation depends upon a balance be-

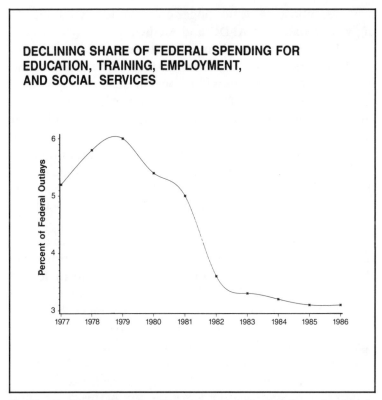

DECLINING SHARE OF FEDERAL SPENDING FOR EDUCATION, TRAINING, EMPLOYMENT, AND SOCIAL SERVICES

Figure 11: Under Reagan, the share of federal dollars devoted to developing the skills of our work force fell dramatically.

Source: U.S. Office of Management and Budget, *The Budget of the United States, Historical Tables*, Fiscal Year 1988, Table 3.1.

tween unity and diversity. The national government should take responsibility for overall direction and program coordination. It should ensure that minimum standards are maintained while it assists the states financially and helps them promote the innovations and achieve the greater responsiveness that comes from being closer to the people and their problems. Once the national government assumes the costs of health and welfare for the poor and needy, the states will save tens of billions of dollars annually. These are not central government dollars donated to the states subject to the whims of Washington budgeters. Rather, they are state revenues whose use is no longer commanded by the matching requirements of AFDC and Medicaid.

Under a new federal compact, the national government would assume much greater responsibility for the health and welfare of the poor, removing from the states a major drain on their expenditures. The states, in turn, would assume the burden for programs to improve human resources and foster economic development, devoting their savings to education, manpower training, job creation, child care, and other social services. Thus, the federal government would deal with the short-run concerns of family impoverishment, while the states would deal with the longer-run concerns of social and economic improvement.

The purpose of the new compact is to define more clearly and better perform two related but different functions: the allocation of broad entitlements that are uniform for all qualifying individuals, and the provision of specific human services attentive to an individual's needs and centered in the individual's home community. The levels of government closest to the people should be the levels most aware of the challenges involved in education and training efforts and should be most capable of innovative approaches to program design and implementation. Greater effort in this area should result in fewer individuals falling into the national safety net. It should also result in a higher-quality work force, better adapted to modern industrial technologies. The states are thus given a fundamental role in regenerating American productivity and in ensuring to every American the opportunity to fully participate in it. The new federal compact is therefore integral to the overall project of Growth with Fairness.

By the terms of this new federal compact, the states' savings must be spent on human services and economic development. Yet the states would have, within broad national guidelines, considerable flexibility as to its specific allocation and discretion over program management. In addition, the central government would maintain a system of categorical grants to provide incentives for the states to recognize the special requirements of the underprivileged, handicapped, and disadvantaged. As federalism, the new compact would achieve a reasonable synthesis of national leadership and local jurisdiction. As public policy, it would put greater government energy into investment in the education and training of America's work force. A society that refuses to invest sufficiently in its citizens will soon find that those citizens are unable to support themselves and unprepared to contribute to that society's prosperity. In the area of social and human resources policy, the new federal compact addresses education, job training, and social services.

Education is the ticket to the future. The level of illiteracy in our country is appalling. The school dropout rate—more than one million a year—is indicative of our failure. The Reagan administration has attacked the public school system but has done nothing to improve it. We must now replace demoralization with determination. For two centuries, free public education has been at the core of the American vision of equal opportunity. It is essential that we provide all young men and women with the knowledge and skills necessary to fulfill their highest potential and to participate usefully in a modern, dynamic, and productive economy.

For preschool children, the Head Start program seeks to better prepare youngsters from disadvantaged backgrounds for the school years ahead, supplementing the family as a source of nurture and remedying educational deficiencies as early as possible. The program now serves nearly 500,000 children per year, but only one-quarter of those who are eligible; thus, it has to be expanded. For primary school children, there is the need to follow through with special educational programs in reading and mathematics. We must improve our ability to diagnose and treat learning handicaps so as to prevent later dropouts, crime, and welfare dependency. We must devote more resources to the training of better-qualified teachers, and we must expand school facilities to reduce tragic overcrowding.

For secondary school children, we must establish minimum standards for graduation and ensure that all students have the ability to solve everyday problems in our increasingly technological society. For those going on to college, the Growth with Fairness program would extend student loans and grants to all those who are academically capable and need financial assistance. For those choosing not to go to college, the program would have the states give greater priority to quality vocational education. It would also call on the federal government to work with the states and the private sector to design a national program to guarantee to every high school graduate either a job or the opportunity to enroll in a truly effective job training program. This is already the law in Great Britain, giving students an extra incentive to finish high school and allowing them to anticipate successful entry into the labor force.

America must increase its efforts at job training, linking them directly to productive employment in the private sector. An expanding market will create opportunities for many individuals who are currently unemployed or underemployed. Yet rising demand has to be matched by adequate supply. We must be sure that America has a fully capable work force and that young workers have the skills that will return the United States to a competitive position in the world economy. We must make special efforts to retrain older workers dispossessed by the changing character of domestic production. In addition, we have an obligation to improve the life chances of those persons at the bottom of the job market, who consistently suffer low wages and demeaning tasks without the prospect for improvement and who are the most vulnerable to layoffs in times of economic fluctuation. And particular attention must be given to the needs of welfare mothers, minority teenagers who face unemployment rates more than triple the norm, and workers living in economically depressed areas. We must break the cycle of dismissal, dependency, discouragement, and delinquency that leaves so many of our citizens without hope.

Three-quarters of the individuals who will be working in the year 2000 are already in the work force. By that time, however, between 5 and 15 million manufacturing jobs will demand different skills while a similar number of service jobs will become obsolete. Even today, about 1.5 million workers are permanently displaced each year and require assistance upon reentering the job market. Approximately a third of our displaced workers are deemed functionally illiterate. Repeated studies have shown that an investment in human resources now will yield a substantial return later. Yet the Reagan administration ended all Public Service Employment, terminating jobs for more than 300,000 persons, fewer than half of whom found alternative employment. It also lowered the number of teenagers enrolled in the Job Corps and sharply reduced spending for placement services. Instead, the administration put greater reliance upon private business, shifting job training authority to Private Industry Councils. Unfortunately, businesses interested in maximizing profits tend to skim off the most capable workers and thus give less assistance in the cases of challenging need.

The states have rapidly expanded their own efforts to fill the job training gap. Thirty-nine states fund customized training programs, most of which target new and expanding firms. These programs adapt their training to the specific skills needed by the firm, and in exchange the firm provides on-the-job experience and often agrees to preferential hiring of trainees. Such customized programs would be enormously expanded under the Growth with Fairness plan. Nevertheless, narrow vocational aims by themselves are not sufficient. Skills necessary today may well be obsolete tomorrow. We must also devote more energy to training the whole individual, giving him or her the ability to prosper in a modern labor market regardless of the changing technological conditions of work. We must better develop the basic capacities of our workers, for these return a payoff over the course of an entire lifetime.

Along with education and job training come the family, social, and community services necessary to help individuals take advantage of their opportunities. We must, for example, significantly improve the quantity and quality of day care in America. According to the Children's Defense Fund, more than 60 percent of today's mothers are in the labor force. More than 9 million children under 6 years old, and more than 14 million children between ages 6 and 13, have working mothers, most of whom are employed full time.

The need for adequate child care is overwhelming. Without it, millions of children become candidates for maltreatment and neglect. In Maine, one study found that hundreds of children under age five spent some time during a typical week caring for themselves. Thousands of children under five were sometimes left alone at home with only a neighbor or friend looking in on them. Child care is essential in the effort to gain equal rights for women, giving working women choices where now they face only constraints. It is also a key prerequisite in the fight against poverty, especially given the huge number of poor female-headed households. Surveys show that a large percentage of the single mothers not currently in the labor force would work if day care were available at reasonable cost; many of those working part time would be glad to work longer hours. Instead they now face a cruel dilemma. An employee, for example, working full time at a minimum wage job earns $6,700 per year. Child care at the below-average price of $1 an hour will cost $2,000 per year. Either the mother accepts a 30 percent drop in a disposable income already well beneath the poverty line, or she quits work and relies entirely on AFDC. The goal to replace welfare with workfare can be made practical only when we provide suitable care for dependent children.

In Sweden, nearly half of all preschool children with parents working or studying have places in the municipal system of child care. In the United States in 1981, child care programs supported by federal grants served only 472,000 children, a paltry figure when compared with 3.4 million children younger than six living in poverty. As a result of President Reagan's budget cuts, funds for such programs were 28 percent lower in 1986 than they were in 1981. Nearly half the states have had to cut back the number of children served by government-supported day care. Many others have maintained their levels only by chopping back services, lowering quality, and sacrificing standards. In the absence of suitable and low-cost facilities, millions of America's working families must rely on a patchwork system including relatives, babysitters, and unlicensed nurseries run out of private homes. As the Children's Defense Fund correctly argues, our federal, state, and local government must take the initiative to build a more effective child care system. A much greater government commitment to child care can ensure that low-income parents and their children get the supportive care they need. The funds made available through this proposed new federal compact should make an important contribution in this critical area.

Child care is just one in a range of services that government provides in the attempt to bring all individuals into the mainstream of economic life. The Growth with Fairness program envisions a network of social services administered by state and local governments, often in cooperation with voluntary organizations but operating according to federal standards and guidelines. The block grants offered by the national government to support these services have all been severely slashed during the Reagan years. It can be anticipated that communities will actively expand and improve their service commitments with funds retained under the federal compact.

In addition to expanding social services, the new federal compact would assign to the states and local governments primary responsibility for necessary job creation. Federal programs to assist small businesses, through the Economic Development Administration and the Community Development Block Grants programs, would be restricted to targeted special-needs groups. In general, states would be encouraged to continue the innovation and experimentation in promoting economic development that has characterized the last decade. Venture capital funds, set-aside programs, mature industry adaptation programs, equity loan programs, industrial incubators, industrial parks, dedication of pension funds to local investment—these are the kinds of efforts that have proliferated in recent years. The Urban Institute study "Economic Development in the Post-Federal Era" recommends increasing the responsibility of the states for economic development. The Growth with Fairness program incorporates this allocation of authority. Of course, the state efforts will require, as discussed in chapter 2, an appropriate federal supporting role, and that is the federal obligation under this compact. This division of responsibilities in economic development should complement the new division of responsibilities envisioned for social welfare and social services.

The ultimate goal of social policy is to help people achieve economic self-sufficiency. It is here that public education, job training, child care, and social services make their contribution. A growing aggregate GNP, founded upon renewed investment in American productive facilities and upon competitive markets in which to sell our goods, will enable many individuals to complete the transition on their own. Nevertheless, to contend that a thriving U.S. economy is essential does not imply that government is irrelevant. This is the logical mistake made by the Reagan administration. It tried to make us believe that the state and the marketplace are antagonistic, that the public sector detracts from private initiative instead of complementing it, that government is always a burden on our backs and never a helping hand. The administration therefore felt free to cast federal responsibilities off to the states while denying the states the funds adequate to maintain them. We cannot just wish for a skilled labor force; we must create it using all the instruments at our command. We cannot just wish that all Americans were able to pursue market opportunities; we must be willing to assist them when necessary, tailoring policies to meet their particular needs.

Americans have always believed that suitable employment helps to realize the potential inherent to every individual and gives to that individual a sense of importance and self-worth. It is a foundation of a stable society as much as of a productive society. Every community has a wealth of individual potential waiting to be useful. Government must begin to experiment with creative and flexible labor market approaches that will get more people into adequately paying permanent jobs in the private sector. The states can be expected, as part of the new federal compact, to welcome this responsibility.

Human resources programs for America's future require innovative leadership. That is why a new federal partnership is proposed here. Such programs require money. That is why this program would increase the funds available to the states by making the federal government responsible for the safety net. In return there would be savings. Part of the financial cost would be recouped through higher tax revenues and lower welfare costs. Yet the most important savings are less material and tangible. We would save individuals their hope and their self-esteem. We would save them the opportunity for full participation in a U.S. economy characterized by growth with fairness.

Fairness for All

Fairness is not a matter for the poor and underprivileged alone; it affects the lives of every one of us. Statistics show that the middle-class lifestyle has deteriorated in recent years. The first half of the post–World War II era was a period of great prosperity and rapidly rising family income. Between 1967 and 1985, by contrast, real income for the average family with children fell by 6.6 percent. Families up through the 80th percentile experienced real income losses; only the richest fraction gained. Today, young heads of households can no longer share the expectations of an affluent future that drove previous generations to work and strive. For example, on average men passing from age 25 to age 35 before 1973 saw their real incomes more than double; since 1973 incomes in the same age group have grown by only 16 percent. The young families of today can no longer anticipate owning their own home or providing a suitable cushion for retirement. They have tried to cope by delaying children, increasing the number of two-earner households, and incurring substantial installment debts. The historic American dream that each succeeding generation will live better than its parents has suffered in recent years. We are in danger of losing the fundamental character that defines us as a people, of losing that venturesome spirit that has been at the foun-

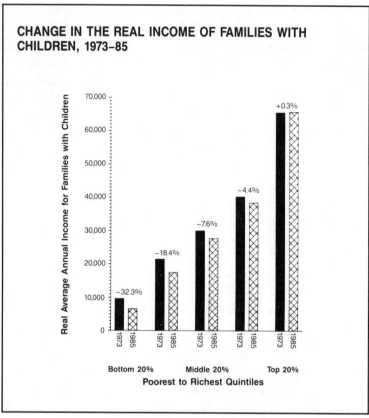

CHANGE IN THE REAL INCOME OF FAMILIES WITH CHILDREN, 1973–85

Figure 12: Between 1973 and 1985, the average real income of families with children declined for every quintile of the population except the richest. Overall, for all families with children, real income declined by 6.6 percent. During this period of stagnation and decline, America's income distribution became more unequal as the poorest Americans suffered the greatest decline in income while the richest gained slightly.

Source: Sheldon Danziger and Peter Gottschalk, "Target Support at Children and Families," *New York Times*, March 22,1987, Business Section, p. 2.

dation of our success.

A badly skewed distribution of income and wealth threatens to create out of the single American nation a two-class society, the rich and the poor, further threatening the American dream. Sixty percent of the population earns only one-third of the income generated annually; that same 60 percent possesses virtually no net wealth. For most Americans, any assets they have in the form of home ownership and savings are more than offset by the liabilities they have incurred. This picture had been relatively stable since the end of World War II. Yet in the short period of the Reagan administration the distribution grew noticeably more uneven. Families in the bottom quintile of the income distribution lost nearly 8 percent of their income between 1981 and 1984; by contrast, those in the top quintile gained nearly 9 percent. This is the equivalent of a $25 billion transfer from the poor to the rich.

Part of the regressive shift in income shares can be blamed directly on Reagan administration policies. More than ever before, jobs have been lost and plants have been closed, destroying people's livelihoods and communities. The new jobs created often impose lower wages, poorer working conditions, and fewer chances for mobility. It has become harder to ensure reasonable stability for oneself and one's family. An Urban Institute simulation shows that a less regressive budget and macroeconomic policy would have resulted in higher real disposable incomes for the bottom 80 percent of American families and lower real disposable income only for the top 20 percent.

The federal government must actively commit itself to designing and implementing laws that attend to the structure and not just the amount of economic activity, that show concern at the personal as well as the broad aggregate level, and that seek to improve overall productivity in ways that are sure to expand and diffuse individual well-being. A great many public policies can contribute to improved economic fairness for the average American worker. The principal emphasis in this section is on regulation. Government can specify our standards for acceptable conduct and stipulate that certain practices are to be prohibited. Such regulations are usually enforced through the legal process, not the budget. They are the main way in which we supervise relations in the private market and ensure that employees are treated justly. Only a few of these regulations and standards are mentioned here, grouped into three general categories.

The first category of regulations concerns conditions of work. Americans should be able to feel confident that they can secure a reasonable job that uses their talents, pays a decent wage, and provides a safe and healthy working environment. Our performance falls well short of these standards. An unemployment rate that falls below 6 percent only in the fifth year of economic upswing is neither normal nor satisfactory. Some level of joblessness is natural to a dynamic economy, as firms rise or decline and people leave their current occupations to seek better prospects. Yet other advanced industrial countries do significantly better, and so can we. Our policymakers have been too willing to accept the market rather than the social definition of full employment. Similarly, the federal minimum wage should be raised by a series of quick steps from the prevailing, disgraceful level of $3.35 an hour up to $5 an hour. As a result of opposition from the White House, the minimum wage has remained unchanged since 1981, the longest period without revision since its original enactment nearly 50 years ago. In 1986, an individual working full time—eight hours a day for 50 weeks a year— at a minimum wage job earned an annual income that was two-thirds of the poverty rate for a household of four. More than 5 million American workers are paid that little. A sizable increase in the minimum wage will have but a miniscule effect on the number of jobs available. It is the most effective single measure to boost the incomes of the working poor. It should be enacted without delay.

In the workplace itself, employees should know that laws protecting their health and safety are being rigorously enforced. Moreover, they should be treated with the respect inherent in a democratic society. Workers do not abandon the basic rights of citizenship during the one-third of each day they spend on the job. This includes the rights not just of speech and organization, but also of participation in the decisions that affect their interests. Arbitrary power and excessive hierarchy are not merely demeaning, they are also unproductive. Repeated studies have shown that the worker who is involved in the workplace and is consulted about its oper-

---

**CORPORATE AMERICA
AND THE AMERICAN STANDARD OF LIVING**

For many years, spokesmen for corporate America boasted that the efficiency of their management produced for American workers the world's highest wages, which in turn permitted American workers to buy the products of American factories and thus to enjoy the world's highest standard of living. Now, apparently, their position has changed. Businessmen have been intimating that, if America is to regain its industrial competitiveness, it must become a low-wage country. Stanley Mihelick, executive vice president of Goodyear, put the matter most explicitly. As he was quoted in the *New York Times* of October 13, 1987, "Unless we get real wages much closer to those of the Brazils and Koreas, we cannot pass along productivity gains to wages and still be competitive." Real wages in Korea and Brazil are about 25 percent of the U.S. level. Does this mean that the wages and living standards of U.S. workers must fall by something like 75 percent before we can regain our international competitiveness? Is this what has become of the American dream during the Reagan era? If this should come to pass, how many American workers would be able to own automobiles? And how many tires would Goodyear be able to sell to American consumers?

---

ation both gives higher output and experiences greater job satisfaction. American industry has for too long functioned with antiquated management techniques based on the sharp separation of mental from physical labor. Such a conception is a continuing constraint on our efforts to improve competitiveness and is antithetical to the American way of life.

The second category of regulations to promote economic fairness concerns the rules by which the market operates. Ours is a free enterprise system that depends for its success upon fair and competitive markets. On the side of business, monopoly practices, insider trading schemes, and other means for the undue restraint of trade are anathema that substitute power relationships in place of the normal equilibrating process of supply and demand. They distort market outcomes, increase inefficiency, and raise consumer prices. The federal government must become more forceful in rooting out such practices to ensure that the American economy operates for the benefit of all. On the side of workers, the federal government must undertake, once again, the vigilant enforcement of the laws, executive orders, court decisions, and administrative rulings that outlaw all forms of discrimination based on race, gender, age, and handicaps. The Reagan administration slashed budget appropriations for civil rights enforcement throughout the government. It lowered the number of actions initiated and lawsuits filed, despite a 50 percent increase in individual complaints. It greatly reduced the backlog of cases pending before the Equal Employment Opportunity Commission by means of an enormous increase in the number of summary "no cause" judgments. It silenced criticisms by the U.S. Commission on Civil Rights by firing half the members. According to the Reagan administration, discrimination exists only when a flagrant violation occurs against specified individuals that is the clear result of conscious intent. According to the Reagan administration, compliance with the law even in those cases of proven discrimination should proceed through voluntary consent.

An administration, by its actions and inactions, sets a tone for the country at large. All seven previous post–World War II presidents, whatever their political party, sought to deepen and expand the federal government's commitment to civil rights and equal employment opportunity. Reagan, however, has signaled to employers that further civil rights progress is not a high national priority. Partly as a consequence, minorities have lost ground during the 1980s. The real income of Black families, even after controlling for household composition, has declined relative to that of Whites. The task before future presidents has been made more difficult. We as a nation must not merely regain the ground that has been lost, but also restore our conviction that much territory remains before us on the road to basic social justice.

The third category of action to increase fairness for all concerns the economic relationships occurring outside the workplace. Individuals do not live merely to produce and exchange. They want to provide for themselves and their families a sufficient quantity of useful commodities, and to enjoy them in a pleasant environment and a secure community. The federal government has a responsibility to advance those common interests that make American society more than the sum of its parts. It must begin again to enforce the laws that protect the natural environment and that control the level of air and water pollution and secure the public health from toxic emissions. It must ensure the safety of consumer products, require fair labeling practices, and institute deterrent penalties for fraud and deception in interstate commerce. It must help establish stable communities at all income levels, with good and affordable housing, convenient transportation, and suitable parks and recreation facilities.

In addition, national legislation is needed to protect communities against the devastating effects of sudden plant closings and to help the affected employees make the transition to other forms of productive employment. Workers and communities should be given advance notice of any impending closing of a major place of employment, and they should be assisted in their efforts to maintain productive facilities under alternative ownership schemes. The equities built up by managers and workers in pension plans and health programs should be protected by law against misappropriation or artificial bankruptcies. Whereas businesses often calculate on the basis of their own short-run profit and loss, the social impact of their choices is very much wider and must be introduced into business decision making. Unscrupulous, runaway firms should be held accountable for the costs they impose on the communities they have deserted. The remainder, who are the vast majority, should be encouraged through cooperative measures to act in ways that are socially responsible.

Conclusion

This chapter has presented a program for fairness that is comprised of three basic parts: a greater federal government role, financial and programmatic, in maintaining the health and welfare safety net; a new compact with the states to increase investment in the nation's human resources; and a more vigorous effort to protect the economic rights of all Americans. Each component uses a different means and addresses a different set of needs. Transfer payments would assist those in poverty, especially the elderly and families with young children, to obtain a subsistence level of income; the federal government would assume primary responsibility for these payments and eliminate the currently unequal treatment of equally destitute individuals. Social services would help reduce the number of the poor, providing the education, job training, and child care necessary to encourage individual self-sufficiency; state governments would assume primary responsibility for these human resources programs to maximize administrative flexibility and policy experimentation. Government regulations would set minimum standards for economic behavior to insure every participant the opportunity to share in the benefits of market growth; enforcement would rely primarily on legal authority.

This three dimensional approach to fairness is not particularly novel. American public policy has always recognized the need for transfers, social services, and regulatory standards, which together combine to form an integrated attack on economic inequity. Over the past few years, we as a society have done less along each of these dimensions than we should, and less than other, comparable advanced industrial nations. The result has been the sacrifice of both equity and the human resources necessary for growth. The program for Growth with Fairness thus calls for a renewed national dedication to a reasonable quality of life for all Americans, and it advances certain innovative proposals for expanded and improved policy impact. We must reverse the attitude of selfish indifference fostered by the Reagan administration. We must accept the critical role government plays in helping to create in America society that grants each individual the economic opportunity and personal respect that he or she deserves.

Chapter 5:

BUDGET AND FISCAL POLICY

This book has presented an economic program for equitable and sustainable growth. That program consists of a set of linked policies: 1) an industrial reconstruction policy built around the creation of an Industrial Development Bank chartered to invest in companies that commit themselves to plans for technological modernization, job creation, and international competitiveness, and around the greater use of public works to rebuild America's decaying physical infrastructure; 2) an international trade policy built around for selective defense of those industries targeted as candidates for short-term modernization tariffs; and 3) a social and human resources policy built around a new federal compact, in which the central government assumes primary responsibility for the health and welfare safety net, while the states dedicate themselves to improving individual potential through education, manpower training, day care, and innovative job creation programs. Underlying this approach is the belief that growth and fairness are compatible principles, that retrenchment is not an acceptable solution to the nation's current problems, and that government must accept an active role in the partnership of public and private sectors so as to revitalize America's productive capacities.

All of this entails a dramatic shift in direction for budgetary and fiscal policy. The Reagan administration fostered much illusion regarding the true size and scope of the federal government. It distorted spending priorities and undermined the government's ability to perform those tasks that properly fall to it. It slashed taxes in an inequitable manner and acted irresponsibly by sanctioning the largest deficits in our history. Its budgets have proven dangerous to the long-term prosperity of the American people.

The Problem: Illusion and Reality

Size of the Tax Burden

In 1900, the total amount of revenue collected by all government in the United States—federal, state, and local—was approximately $1 billion. In 1936, during the middle of the Great Depression, it was $10 billion. The total reached $100 billion in 1956, $500 billion in 1977, and exceeded $1 trillion in 1984. About two-thirds of this amount was collected by the federal government, the remainder by the states and localities. In 1929, the total tax bite out of an 8-hour working day for the average taxpayer was 52 minutes; by 1984, it was 2 hours and 37 minutes. Taxation has grown enormously over the twentieth century, reflecting the additional responsibilities the American people have assigned to government.

The Reagan administration continually told us that we must put a stop to the seemingly inexorable growth of federal taxes. However, contrary to widespread belief, our burdens have changed only slightly during the post–World War II era. Although the dollar amounts have grown exponentially, so too has the size of the U.S. economy, from which those taxes are paid. In FY 1947, the ratio of federal revenues to GNP was 17.2 percent; in FY 1986, it was 18.5 percent. This represents an increase, over a 40-year span, of only 1.3 cents per dollar. The increased aggregate burden from state and local taxes actually has been greater than from federal taxes. There is a popular impression, promoted by Reagan administration rhetoric, that the federal government, under pressure from accelerating welfare commitments, greatly enlarged its tax bite into market earnings starting in the early 1960s and continuing without restraint until forcibly checked in the 1980s. The official budget data, however, does not support this impression. In fact, the range of variation in the ratio of taxes to GNP has been small, the peaks have not been enduring, and the overall trend is minimal.

Moreover, the tax burden in the United States stands very low compared with that in other advanced industrial societies. According to cross-national data, the United States ranked 20th among the 23 OECD countries in 1984, followed only by Spain, Japan, and Turkey. The ratio between the taxes we collected from all sources and the size of our domestic economy was under 30 percent, more than eight points below the OECD average and even further below that of Sweden, Denmark, Belgium, Norway, the Netherlands, and France, all of which exceeded 45 percent. Nor were taxes in the United States among the fastest growing. From 1965 to 1984, the U.S. tax ratio rose by just 2.68 percent of domestic product, as contrasted with a 10.26 percentage point rise in the OECD average. Every government except Turkey expanded more rapidly. Importantly, the comparatively small size of the U.S. tax burden does not appear to be the consequence of Reagan administration policies. The United States also ranked well toward the bottom of the OECD list in 1980, before the so-called Reagan revolution, and the U.S. growth in relative tax burdens between 1965 and 1980 was the slowest of the OECD countries except Finland. There are reasons to be concerned about the level and allocation of taxes in America. Yet the Reagan administration, in focusing its partisan attacks upon the total size of the government, misdirected our attention away from the real problems and toward a spurious one. The historical period popularly characterized as one of uncontrolled expansion in the fiscal size of the U.S. government was, in comparative terms, remarkable for its moderation.

Debt and Deficits

Government expenditures in the post–World War II era did expand somewhat faster than tax receipts, drifting slowly upward under every president, regardless of political party or ideology. As a share of GNP, all government spending rose, between 1947 and 1986, from 20.1 percent to 32.5 percent. For the federal government alone, the rise was from 15.4 percent to 23.8 percent. Nevertheless, this increase is the equivalent of only 2.1 additional cents per dollar per decade. Compared with other nations, the United States again ranks low in government spending at all levels relative to total GNP. While the United States spends just over 30 percent, Germany, Britain, and France each spend over 40 percent, and Sweden spends over 50 percent.

The logical consequence of government expenditures rising faster than revenues is increased deficits and debt. Every year except one since 1961 the federal budget has been in deficit. Although the dollar imbalance has grown over time, it has soared during the Reagan years, surpassing $220 billion in 1986. With recurrent and increasing annual deficits, the total gross federal debt has grown as well. The debt surpassed $250 billion after the end of World War II, $500 billion in 1975, $1 trillion in 1981, and $2 trillion in 1986. In five years, the same Reagan administration that had initially promised balanced budgets managed to double the national debt. Federal interest payments necessary to carry such a debt similarly soared, from $4.2 billion in 1947 to $136 billion in 1986. Whereas net interest charges absorbed between 6 percent and 8 percent of federal outlays from 1952 through 1978, they constituted 13.7 percent in 1986, and the proportion is growing.

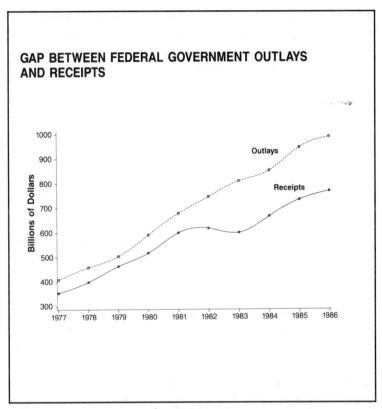

GAP BETWEEN FEDERAL GOVERNMENT OUTLAYS
AND RECEIPTS

Figure 13: Since 1981, there has been an enormous and growing increase in the dollar amount of the federal deficit. The gap between expenditures and revenues ballooned to more than $220 billion in 1986.

Source: Office of Management and Budget, *The Budget of the United States, Historical Tables*, Fiscal Year 1988, Table 1.1.

It is not obvious, however, how such numbers should be interpreted. Like individuals taking out a mortgage, the federal government can reasonably decide to borrow to finance its major capital purchases. Under certain conditions, it might also decide to absorb higher carrying charges to finance current expenditures with high expected returns for growth and fairness. Some of the present deficit can be considered a logical Keynesian corrective to an economy operating well short of its potential. Cross-nationally, the United States has traditionally relied upon deficit spending to a lesser extent than have other advanced industrial societies. Most important, we must remember that the gross federal debt as a share of the total economic product has tended downwards over most of the postwar era. It is now substantially easier to pay off the entire debt, if we should ever choose to do so, than it was during the 1940s and 1950s. In fact, despite its enormous increase in recent years, the gross debt relative to our GNP was 51.2 percent in 1986, approximately the same as during the optimistic Kennedy years of 1963–64.

In particular, the Reagan debt is dangerous because its precipitous rise is a sign of irresponsible fiscal management. Taxes have been slashed regardless of spending commitments. It is dangerous because the nation has to carry substantial present interest payments, and its borrowing has bought items with little prospective future payoff. The combination of regressive tax cuts and large military outlays has contributed virtually nothing to revitalized growth or improved fairness. It is dangerous, most of all, because the debt itself, under prevailing economic conditions, is detrimental to our efforts to rebuild America's productivity capacity. In the presence of enormous consumer and corporate debt and very low domestic savings, high government borrowing only serves to boost interest rates, thereby impairing investment and trade. The pressing issue raised by the deficit, then, is only partly a matter of dollars recorded in federal accounts. Primarily it is a matter of negative economic consequences. The deficit must be reduced to facilitate industrial modernization, growth, and competitiveness.

Budgetary Priorities

The Reagan administration must shoulder most of the responsibility for the debt and deficit problem. Before 1982, the federal deficit exceeded 3 percent of GNP only four times, and these were in years of war or major recession. During the past five years, however, the deficit has averaged 5.2 percent of GNP. The Reagan administration did not initiate the steps necessary to reverse this pattern. Instead, it misdirected national attention by simultaneously proposing both too little and too much. On the one hand, it attacked "big spenders" in the Congress, implying that all problems would cease if other public officials exercised greater control over domestic programs. On the other hand, it sought a balanced budget amendment to the Constitution, implying that recovery will only come with a major revision in our established rules of budgeting. Yet the currently swollen federal deficit does not reflect a failure of either political will or institutional processes. Its origin lies in the distorted budget priorities—the exact mix of military outlays, tax revenues, and social programs—sponsored by the Reagan administration itself. Remedy will come once those priorities are reversed.

Compared with other nations, the United States has been distinctive not just for its relatively low tax burden but also for its high share of defense expenditures contrasted with a very low share for domestic welfare. During the 1960s and 1970s, the United States slowly moved in the direction of the OECD averages for defense and welfare expenditures. This trend was emphatically reversed under Reagan. Between 1981 and 1986, while human and physical resources declined as a share of federal outlays, defense spending climbed from 23.2 percent to 27.6 percent. Over those five years, federal defense outlays increased by $115.9 billion, a rise of 73 percent. This is the single most important reason why expenditures as a share of GNP did not decline under the Reagan administration, but instead were higher on average than under any previous postwar administration. In real terms, military spending between 1981 and 1986 accounted for more than half of the total increase in federal outlays. Moreover, actual military spending has grown less than has been requested in the Reagan administration budget proposals.

A sense of fiscal responsibility demands that a president dedicated to so rapid and expensive a military buildup would seek the additional revenues with which to pay the bills. Just the opposite, the Reagan administration made tax reduction a major government priority and refused to budge despite the obvious need for funds. While federal defense expendi-

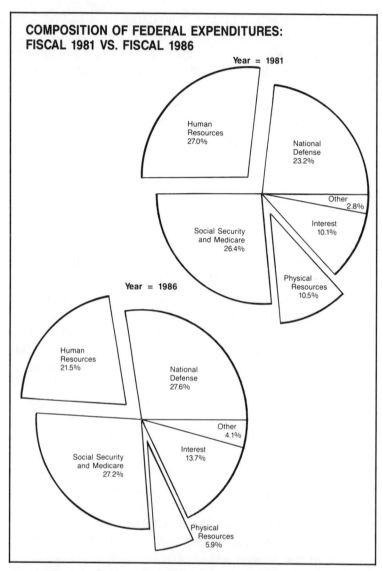

**COMPOSITION OF FEDERAL EXPENDITURES:
FISCAL 1981 VS. FISCAL 1986**

Year = 1981

Human
Resources
27.0%

National
Defense
23.2%

Other
2.8%

Interest
10.1%

Social Security
and Medicare
26.4%

Physical
Resources
10.5%

Year = 1986

Human
Resources
21.5%

National
Defense
27.6%

Other
4.1%

Interest
13.7%

Social Security
and Medicare
27.2%

Physical
Resources
5.9%

Figure 14: The allocation of federal dollars changed substantially during
the Reagan years. The United States now devotes a much greater share
of spending to national defense and interest payments. The main losers
are human resources and physical resources, which are the most
important categories for sustained growth with fairness.

Source: Office of Management and Budget, *The Budget of the United States,
Historical Tables*, Fiscal Year 1988, Table 3.1.

tures between 1981 and 1986 were rising by 1.3 percent of GNP, federal tax receipts were declining by 1.6 percent. Had the federal government collected the same share of revenues in 1986 as in 1981, it would have raised nearly $70 billion more per year, approximately equal to half the net increase in the deficit under Reagan.

In addition, the Reagan tax changes have significantly subverted the historic American principle of progressive taxation based on ability to pay. Contrary to popular illusion, the distribution of tax burdens in the United States in 1980, just prior to the so-called Reagan fiscal revolution, was roughly flat. According to the sophisticated studies of Joseph Pechman, each decile of households ranked by income paid about the same share in taxation. Federal taxes, due to the role of the personal income tax, were slightly progressive; state and local taxes, because of the reliance upon sales taxes, were slightly regressive. Although treatment varied for households within each decile, the net effect was to leave the pretax social distribution of income virtually unchanged. This was the structure of the U.S. tax system so vehemently attacked by Reagan. At the center of his attack was the one clearly progressive piece of the structure, the federal personal income tax. The marginal rate in the top income tax bracket in 1978 was 70 percent. In 1985, it was 50 percent. In 1988, the tax rate for the top income bracket will become only 28 percent.

Moreover, Social Security and other payroll taxes, which are the most burdensome form of tax for the poorest two-fifths of the population, were increased under Reagan. Whereas the share of federal revenues derived from income taxes declined by 2.3 percent between 1981 and 1986, the share derived from social insurance taxes grew by 6.4 percent. Finally, the Reagan administration contributed its bit to the continuing demise of corporate taxation by reducing the basic tax rate for corporations from 46 to 34 percent and significantly liberalizing depreciation allowances. In 1952, the corporate tax supplied nearly a third of all federal revenues. In 1986 it supplied only 8.2 percent. Thus, under Reagan, the financing of the federal government increasingly shifted from the owners of great wealth to the backs of the average working man and woman. The entire U.S. tax system has become more regressive. An inequitable system at the administration's beginning, it has suffered three major new pieces of tax legislation during the 1980s and has emerged even less credible than before. The federal government now has less capacity than ever to raise necessary funds, and in the process, it has most relieved from tax burdens those individuals financially best able to contribute.

With defense up and taxes down, the only way to balance the budget was to strip expenditures on human and physical resources, to cut back on the assistance given by the federal government to the people and the productive facilities of this country. In FY 1986, after the Reagan budget changes, defense absorbed 27.6 percent of $989.8 billion in total federal outlays, leaving $716.6 billion for other purposes. By statute, the interest on the debt ($136.0 billion) had to be paid. By political commitment, Social Security and other retirement programs ($245.5 billion) had to be protected. If just three other programs—Medicare for the elderly, veterans benefits, and unemployment insurance payments—were also protected, the remainder would have been $220.7 billion, a sum exactly equal to the 1986 deficit. To eliminate the deficit with that remainder would have left the federal government with no money for anything else. It could spend nothing on foreign aid and space exploration, on the development of our natural resources, on the maintenance of our national parks, on education and manpower training, on Aid to Families with Dependent Children and Food Stamps, on housing and community development, and on disaster relief. The deficit is due, then, not to any failure of political will, but to the mix of existing policy priorities.

The unprecedented Reagan deficits continue, moreover, despite deep cuts that have already been made in domestic spending programs. The extent of these savings can be assessed through the use of a hypothetical "baseline," the amount that would have been spent had the cuts not been made. According to the Congressional Budget Office, domestic spending relative to the baseline had been slashed through FY 1985 by $56 billion, or 1.5 percent of GNP. These cuts were not across-the-board. They did not affect all programs or population groups equally. Particularly disadvantaged were the working poor and near-poor, who lost not only cash assistance, but also the incentives and institutional supports useful in helping them better themselves. This is the group that, in addition, least benefited from the Reagan tax cuts and most suffered from the slack Reagan economy. A budget reveals the real policy priorities of a presidency stripped of all camouflage and verbiage. In the 1980s, the U.S. federal budget tells the story of shortsighted sacrifices in human and infrastructure investment, of suffering imposed on those least able to bear it, and of an overall disregard for the contributions of public policy to the domestic well-being of the country.

Reducing the Budget Deficit

The history of the Reagan administration is that of the great budget experiment. The administration promised to reduce government burdens and expand the economy. Instead, we got increased militarization and a market-distorting fiscal imbalance. According to the administration, government is nothing but a drain on productive resources. By cutting taxes and raising the marginal return on work, savings, and investment, it maintained that enormous economic energy would magically be unleashed from artificial restraint, generating enough new output to restore competitiveness, guarantee well-paying jobs for a growing population, and still maintain the public safety net and finance a huge rise in defense expenditures. The experiment has been a failure. Promising to sacrifice distributional fairness in exchange for higher national economic growth, it has left the nation with neither.

Yet the Reagan administration emphatically refused to retreat from its supply-side litany or to admit that internal contradictions beset its budgetary experiment. Rather than confront the dilemma of reconciling higher military spending with sweeping tax cuts, the administration consistently sought to shift the buck. An administration that produced the largest budget deficits in our history hypocritically urged a balanced budget amendment that reflects a profound distrust of the democratic process and of our representative institutions.

The call for greater fiscal responsibility has become an accepted item on the present American political agenda. It should be, but with a major qualification. There are good and bad ways to be responsible. The wrong way is to assume that if government officials simply pay attention to the prudent management of public finances, the private market will take care of itself. A better way is to note that the budget is an important instrument in the repertory of government policy and that its adjustments can be helpful in promoting economic growth and stability. Within that repertory, a reduction in the budget deficit is currently necessary. Necessary, however, is not the same as sufficient. There is no mechanical budget number that will automatically restore American productive competitiveness. It is not enough for government to regulate the broad financial taps and leave the response to the private market. Exclusive attention to the aggregate deficit can easily lead to indiscriminate expenditure cuts or tax increases. This has been the experience under Gramm-Rudman-Hollings. If enacted by the criterion of political convenience, indiscriminate spending cuts might well burden those least capable of defending themselves. If justified simply by identifying deficit reduction with the nation's economic prosperity, indiscriminate cuts might well sacrifice essential government programs. Blind quantification will achieve neither acceptable growth nor fairness. Just as deficit reduction must be evaluated by its effect on the way Americans produce and consume, so must all of the parts that make up the budget. There are some tough decisions to be made in the years ahead. Yet, in an effort to cut the deficit and undo the damage Reagan wrought, it would be wrong not to build a solid foundation for the future.

By contrast with Reagan administration economics, the Growth with Fairness fiscal policy is based on three simple premises. First, it is absolutely essential to shrink the federal budget deficit, thus lowering interest rates, releasing savings for productive investment, and helping readjust international financial markets. Second, federal programs that play an essential role in national economic life must be expanded to provide the essential underpinnings of private market success. Third, to shrink the deficit and extend needed programs, it is obligatory that we generate additional revenues, fairly and efficiently.

The fiscal program advanced here to meet the needs of Growth with Fairness contains $35 billion more in deficit reduction. This amount is both practical and effective. It will make a significant dent in the federal deficit but without unnecessary disturbances to other parts of the government budget or to financial markets. An additional $35 billion, for example, would lower the deficit for FY 1987 by 25 percent below the official Office of Management and Budget prediction, and it would reduce the gross federal debt by close to 1 percent of GNP. A strong commitment to deficit reduction will signal to investors in federal securities that our government is firmly on the road to restoring reason to the management of its financial accounts. Further, it will help reassure our creditors, making it easier to sell new obligations and diminishing the possibility of a dangerous loss of confidence. Finally, it will help relieve some of the pressure that government borrowing places on capital markets, reducing the overall interest rate while making more investment funds available for private industrial expansion. A lower federal deficit is a pressing national need, essential to the rejuvenation of American competitiveness.

This plan for Growth with Fairness also calls for $35 billion in additional federal expenditures for investment in our physical and economic infrastructure, and for $35 billion more for investment in human development and welfare reform. To raise the revenues required to finance these added expenditures necessary to rebuild industrial America, this program proposes two significant spending cuts—in wasteful military outlays and in subsidies to large corporate agriculture—and four tax initiatives—an excise on luxury consumption, a levy on speculation in secondary securities, the retention of some measure of progressivity in the federal income tax, and an increase in the taxes paid by the estates of the wealthy.

It would have been easier politically just to propose the deficit reduction. The argument of this book, however, is that the country cannot afford to do so little. In the long run, a budget based on mere cutting back will be less secure than one based on going forward. It is necessary to integrate greater budget responsibility into a broader program designed to reinvigorate the national economy. Deficit reduction, therefore, must be seen as only one prong in a multipronged effort to return America to the forefront among the advanced industrial societies.

Revenues for Growth with Fairness

To be fiscally responsible, the Growth with Fairness program for rebuilding America's future requires $105 billion in additional funds. The issue is how to raise them, from whom, and by what justification. Two principles have guided the choice of revenue sources to finance the program outlined in this book: 1) that we hurt least those who can least afford to be hurt, and 2) that we discourage behavior that adversely affects our national well-being and in turn encourage behavior that contributes to the rebuilding of American productive capacity. Growth and fairness are not applicable only to the expenditure side of the budget. They must govern the revenue side as well. Sound finance requires that we subtract from certain public outlays and extract from certain private incomes. In every case, however, needed funds will be secured from policy changes that are justified by their effect on overall social justice and economic prosperity.

Defense and the Military Budget

The American people realize the necessity of a strong, robust, and resilient national defense. One of the most important changes occurring at the end of World War II was the abandonment of isolationism and the emergence of bipartisan agreement on the importance of engagement with the other countries of the world. We wanted this engagement to be constructive and peaceful, but we were ready to defend our national interests militarily if ever the need should arise. As a consequence of the failure in Vietnam, American public opinion demanded a reduction in our military spending. Between 1971 and 1978, defense outlays declined in real terms by almost 25 percent. For the first time since the demobilization following World War II, they absorbed less than 5 percent of the GNP. Meanwhile, the Soviet Union was perceived to be investing heavily in new armaments. That, as well as the debacle in Iran and the conflict in Afghanistan, prompted a review of our defense posture and resulted, in 1979, in an ambitious effort by the Carter administration to upgrade and modernize our weaponry.

The Reagan administration then took this emerging trend and dangerously exaggerated it. Obsessed with the specter of Soviet expansionism, the president declared that the sky would be the limit for the weapons buildup he would sponsor and implement. Accepting as gospel truth the worst-case scenarios about the capabilities and intentions of the Soviets, Reagan offered the armed forces a virtual carte blanche to convert their wish lists of expensive gadgetry into weapons programs incorporated into the military budget. Through 1981–86, defense expenditures grew by more than $115 billion, by more than 41 percent after controlling for inflation. Military spending became the absolute top priority over all the other purposes of government, the only constraint being the willingness of Congress to appropriate the funds.

The Reagan administration's frantic peacetime buildup of sophisticated weaponry was never based on a coherent set of assumptions or objectives about the strategic purposes that these weapons systems would serve. There was little coordination between the different branches of the armed services. There was a confusing preference for the long-run development of technological hardware over the short-run operational readiness of American forces. So much money was spent so hastily that contracts were let prematurely to eager defense contractors regardless of poor design and incomplete testing. The consequences were enormous waste, sloppy procurement methods, lax administration, and defective quality control. This was not just a matter of overpriced coffee pots and toilet seats, which made lurid headlines in recent years. Billions of dollars were literally thrown away on such lemons as the Sergeant York divisional air defense system, which the Pentagon finally canceled after it was deemed an operational failure, and on the Bradley fighting vehicle, which is still in the budget despite being more vulnerable to antiarmor attack than its predecessor and despite its proven difficulties in crossing rivers and streams under combat conditions.

Even more wasteful has been the mindless accumulation of very costly weapons systems that duplicate existing ones but have no clear or distinctive strategic advantage. A few examples will illustrate this point. The $15 billion land-based MX nuclear missile system was muscled through a reluctant Congress despite an array of virtually 7,000 submarine-based strategic missiles and airborne cruise missiles that provide a more than adequate basis for our second-strike deterrent. The Reagan administration also sought to add 42 more of these immobile MX missiles, supplemented by $45 billion for 500 smaller "Midgetmen." Most experts doubt that such a marginal and vulnerable addition to U.S. retaliatory capability would in any way further convince the Soviets not to launch a strike against the continental United States.

The B-1 manned bomber, priced at $200 million per aircraft, is rapidly becoming the Edsel of the Air Force. Defects already encountered in avionics, flight control, and low-flying radar make it unlikely that this complex plane would ever be able to penetrate Soviet air defenses. The whole notion of a manned nuclear attack bomber long ago should have been declared as obsolete as the cavalry horse. Instead, the Reagan administration persisted with further modifications of the B-1 and proceeded with plans to build a new and enormously more expensive generation of manned bombers using ultra top-secret "Stealth" technology.

The appetite of the Navy continues to grow as well. The Navy dreams of a 600-ship fleet and of two additional carrier groups, the latter at a price tag of $40 billion. Carrier aircraft are the most vulnerable and most costly way of delivering air power. The Navy persists in giving high priority to offensive operations, as opposed to the vital but less glamorous task of antisubmarine warfare, which is essential to the defense of intercontinental sealanes.

Finally, the Reagan administration's obsession with the Strategic Defense Initiative (Star Wars) program is irrational and dangerous. Its astronomical cost has been estimated at $1 trillion over 10 years. Overwhelming scientific evidence that it could not fully protect us from hostile nuclear attack did not inhibit the president from continuing with this strategic fantasy. Even as a partial air defense system, it violates our ABM treaty obligations and would have a destabilizing effect on the delicate balance of international deterrence.

Beyond its exorbitant budgetary price, the hidden costs of this escalation of defense spending must not be overlooked. In the long run, it contributes to the further undermining of our industrial productivity and competitiveness. Many of our best scientists, engineers, and highly skilled workers are being diverted to work on military projects with small civilian economic return. More than 30 percent of American research and development funds are absorbed by the military, compared with 1 percent in Japan and less than 10 percent in Germany. The aggregate demand multiplier, indicating the diffusion of purchases and the stimulation of jobs throughout the U.S. economy, appears lower for military outlays than for the ordinary dollar of government spending. Military hardware helps little in rectifying our international trade imbalance and offers nothing to domestic civilian consumption.

The president who so emphatically denounced the pork-barrel politics of domestic public works and social welfare programs has opened the flood gates to even greater pork-barrel politics through swollen defense budgets. The president who so forcefully condemned government interference with the free market economy has introduced significant new market distortions that will limit our capacity to grow. Apparently President Reagan believes that the nation can suffer economic ills only from the domestic side of the budget and that anything can be sacrificed in the name of defense. In fact, the relationship tends to go the other way. National security requires far more than stockpiles of sophisticated weapons. No sound military structure can be built on the foundation of an undereducated citizenry or a weak economy, both of which have been neglected in recent years by the administration's single-minded fixation on accumulating the latest hardware.

In 1985, the Reagan administration projected increases in defense budget authority that would have approached half a trillion dollars annually by the early 1990s. This was too much for Congress and the country to swallow. Despite bitter protests and prophesies of disaster from defense establishment spokesmen and industrial contractors, the military procurement bonanza has run out of steam. Congress has begun to reassert control over spending. The White House is now prepared to settle for $312 billion by 1990, and the Congress has indicated its determination to hold the level at $290 billion. This return to sanity in our national security planning is welcome. Yet it is possible to go further.

As the primary concern of this book is economic policy, a more specific discussion of the available choices for reduction among advanced weaponry is not laid out. Careful, detailed, and well-informed analyses can be found in studies already published by the Brookings Institution and the Committee for National Security. Here, the focus is the budget and the reasonable savings that can be gained through adjustments that in no way impair our national defense. Those savings are significant.

The Growth with Fairness fiscal plan calls for Congress to reduce new obligational authority for the national defense budget by $40 billion per year for each of the next four fiscal years. No new major weapons systems should be authorized or funded during this period. This would give the new administration, and the country at large, the opportunity to reassess and redefine our security needs in terms of a systematic analysis of the threats we face. It would also permit the armed forces to learn how to use, adapt, and maintain the sophisticated new arms that are now coming on line. In addition, it should give the United States the opportunity to negotiate binding and mutually enforceable arms control agreements with the Soviet Union. In view of the recent sluggishness of the Soviet economy and the apparent interest of the Gorbachev leadership in arms reduction, the time may be auspicious for new agreements that would enable both sides to reduce their weapons procurement.

Unfortunately, however, $40 billion per year in reduced budget authority does not immediately translate into dollar savings of expenditure outlays. The time lags are enormously long. While most of the funds for the Reagan generation of weapons have been committed, the spending for actual procurement and delivery will extend for another three to five years. The backlog is so great that, even if new budget authority were absolutely zero, defense outlays in 1990 would be more than $200 billion. Major recisions of obligational authority from previous years would involve very costly cancellation fees and other legal penalties, meaning that we are largely locked into what we already have on order. Some spending reductions are possible in the short run, amounting to about $15 billion annually. This is the approximate equivalent of a 5 percent decrease relative to FY 1987 projections. Much greater savings in actual outlays, reflecting changes in weapons planning, would then occur in the third year of this program and would increase over time.

In any discussion of defense costs and expenditures, it is easy to lose our sense of perspective. We become so accustomed to manipulating such huge numbers that we tend to round off any figure below $100 million. When considering a military budget of nearly $300 billion, we lose sight of the fact that the complete package of federal health and welfare benefits to low-income households costs the Treasury less than a third of that amount. Federal spending for education is about 6 percent and revenue sharing with the states is about 2 percent of that amount. We must always remember the trade-offs when considering expensive additions to our weapons technology. From a national security perspective, there is ample leeway for reform without sacrificing our strategic deterrence or combat readiness. From an economic perspective, such reform will release funds for allocation to more productive public sector uses, free talented manpower and resources for employment in the civilian sector, and contribute to a reduction in the budget deficit that should lower the cost of capital for industrial redevelopment. From a budgetary perspective, reform would help reintroduce sanity into the priorities reflected in the budget document, reversing the Reagan administration's predilection for the equipment of destruction over the equitable treatment of individuals. For these reasons, the realm of military expenditures cannot be ignored in the construction of an overall program for Growth with Fairness.

Agriculture Subsidies and the Family Farm

The founders of the our republic believed strongly that an industrious, independent, property-owning class of yeoman farmers would provide the backbone of our new society and would be the most stalwart defenders of democratic government. Since Jefferson, agricultural policy has helped to foster and strengthen the family farm as a cherished institution of American life. The Homestead Act made 160 acres of Western land available to any family that would clear and cultivate it for a period of five years. Land grants set up our state universities dedicated to making the benefits of practical education and science accessible to all farm families. Our network of extension services, farm credit, crop insurance, soil conservation and irrigation aid have helped to make American agriculture the most technologically progressive and productive system the world has ever known.

The history of American agriculture offers two important lessons. First, we as a people have always valued the owner-operated farm both as an efficient mode of commodity production and as a lifestyle with a welcome place in our society. Second, family agriculture has never been a domain of laissez-faire dogmatism. Instead, the federal government has been an active partner, helping these enterprises flourish through a series of pragmatically responsive public services. In this regard, the United States has been a pioneer emulated by nations around the world.

During the course of the twentieth century, however, there have been dramatic changes in the character of American agriculture and agricultural policy. On the one hand, the great efficiency of our farm production led to large commodity surpluses, which had the effect of seriously depressing prices. At the height of the Great Depression, farmers were burning wheat as fuel because it did not pay them to market it, while millions of American families went hungry in the cities. Ironically, the harder the farmers worked and the more food they produced, the lower the prices they received. The New Deal initiated the crop limitation programs upon which subsequent policy has been built. The federal government currently purchases and stores many surplus commodities, and it pays farmers to voluntarily restrict the acreage cultivated. These policies were designed to protect the family farm from some of the natural risks and economic uncertainties inherent in the planting cycle, and to ease the costs of transition as many farm families leave agriculture for higher-paying jobs in the cities. Nevertheless, our agriculture is so fantastically productive that the 3 percent of our labor force remaining in farming is still capable of feeding our entire population while generating large surpluses available for export.

At the same time, the twentieth century has witnessed a spectacular rise in the size of the average farm. The largest 10 percent of farms now control more than half of total sales. Corporations and absentee landlords have increasingly dominated the agricultural sector, gaining control of the farm lobbies and distorting the purposes of government policies in the process. Agribusiness enterprises are in the business of farming, not as a way of life but primarily to win a high rate of return on their capital. Far too often, corporate farmers deplete soils and spoil water supplies in their drive for fast profits, unlike family farmers who must husband their land for it contains their inheritance. Far too often, corporate producers orient their production decisions not to competitive markets, but to maximize price support payments at the taxpayers' expense. Virtually a third of all federal agricultural subsidies accrue to the 4.1 percent of farm units with annual sales exceeding $250 thousand.

We have tended to accept the system of agricultural supports, despite the higher prices and higher taxes they impose, because we share a broad consensus in support of the family-owned and -operated farm. We generally consider reasonable farm subsidies to be a fair price to pay for guaranteed supplies of high-quality foodstuffs. Yet during the last 25 years, our agricultural policies have veered seriously off course. It is intolerable that, of the $26 billion of federal support paid in FY 1986, the main beneficiaries were the largest farm units. It is intolerable, for instance, that the Prince of Liechtenstein receives an unearned $2 million subsidy for his holdings in Texas. The cost is too high and our budget needs are too great for us to continue to subsidize the profitability of corporate agribusiness.

One solution, endorsed by the Reagan administration as part of its mindless free market ideology, is to totally eliminate all price supports. This would subject our family farmers to the mercies of a volatile world market and leave them prey to mounting debt and the threat of foreclosures. In time, most family farms would be swallowed up by their corporate competitors, and the independent yeoman would continue to live only in the pages of our history books. A more practical solution is available. It is absurd to offer generous crop subsidies to all farm units, regardless of type or size. Congress has recently taken some small steps to limit their availability. This policy should go much further.

The Growth with Fairness fiscal plan would make crop subsidy payments fully applicable for only the first $150 thousand of output per farm. Payments would then taper off sharply and terminate at $300 thousand of output. Congress should include in its legislation strong penalties for efforts to evade this reform by subdividing large holdings among dummy corporations or relatives. This Growth with Fairness policy would maintain basic protection for truly family-size farms, continuing to provide them with a more stable market environment, although it would not—nor is it intended to—insulate them from all risks. But it would be a first step toward eliminating government support for gigantic agricultural businesses, which would then be forced to compete in the marketplace without guaranteed profitability from taxpayer dollars. Since there are few, if any, economies of scale in farming, this should have negligible effects on productive efficiency. It would, by contrast, establish strong incentives to promote the kind of farm enterprise treasured by our American ideals, and it would save the federal government billions of dollars from current outlays. This simple reform would reduce annual federal expenditures by approximately $10 billion. That money would be reallocated from corporate agriculture to uses that far better meet the purposes of national economic reinvigoration.

Taxation, Market Incentives, and Progressive Burdens

The object of federal taxation, expressed in scores of textbooks on public finance, is to raise needed revenues and to do so in a manner that promotes distributional equity and economic efficiency. The federal revenue code, an instrument that generates hundreds of billions of dollars annually for the government, can never be totally neutral in its effects. Inescapably, it allocates burdens across the various groups in the population, and it affects the framework of incentives and disincentives in the marketplace. From the beginning, Americans have understood that taxation is a powerful mechanism of public policy. For example, the very first permanent U.S. income tax law of 1913 established a progressive rate structure, with burdens rising in seven steps according to income because it was deemed fairer to tax individuals according to their ability to pay.

The Reagan administration has violated all three of the cannons fundamental to sound public finance: adequate revenues, distributional equity, and economic incentives. First, in the midst of an escalation of military expenditures, its unjustifiable mania for tax cuts slashed federal receipts by approximately 2 percent of GNP, adding nearly $100 billion to the net annual deficit. Second, at a time when the market distribution of earnings was becoming more unequal, its opposition to progressive taxation dramatically subverted the principle of burdens according to ability to pay. According to a Joint Economic Committee study, for example, the 1981 tax bill substantially lowered the tax burden on the richest 10 percent of taxpayers filing joint returns, had little effect on the next 40 percent, and imposed increased burdens on the remaining bottom half of households.

Third, in an era when U.S. productivity was lagging and its competitiveness was falling, the Reagan administration's dogmatic attachment to supply-side mythology led to indiscriminate rate reductions rather than to carefully targeted subsidies designed to direct investment dollars into the most useful channels. It was always unreasonable to believe that simply placing more money in the hands of the wealthy and of corporate businessmen would automatically unleash a torrent of productive investment. The administration's extreme fear of government abuses only produced a diminution of the government's ability to exercise needed leverage, and much of the money no longer collected was thus diverted into luxury consumption or paper speculation. Symbolic of this trend was the 1986 replacement of the investment tax credit, which granted business tax preferences strictly in proportion to the purchase of new productive equipment, with a lower corporate tax rate applicable to all profitable firms, whether investing for the future or not.

The need to restore government revenues, to reestablish rate progressivity, and to ensure efficient market stimulation should call forth yet another major legislative effort at tax reform. Yet the country, tired from three such episodes during the Reagan years, is not now ready for another try. For a while at least, the next U.S. president will have to live with

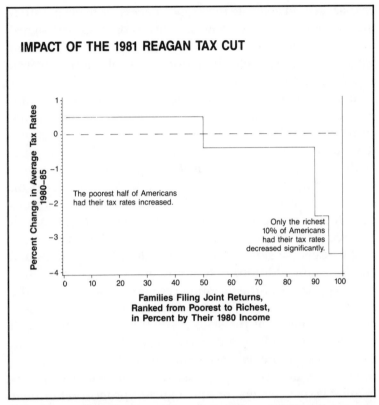

IMPACT OF THE 1981 REAGAN TAX CUT

The poorest half of Americans had their tax rates increased.

Only the richest 10% of Americans had their tax rates decreased significantly.

Families Filing Joint Returns, Ranked from Poorest to Richest, in Percent by Their 1980 Income

Figure 15: The Reagan personal income tax reform of 1981 was a bonanza only for the wealthy. Families were treated differently by the legislation depending on their income. The cuts were most lucrative for the richest 5 percent, were of significant benefit for the next 5 percent, but had little effect on the remainder of families. In fact, tax burdens rose slightly for the bottom half of taxpayers filing joint returns.

Source: Valerie Amerkahail, U.S. Congress, Joint Economic Committee, *Impact of the 1981 Personal Income Tax Reductions on Income Distribution*.

the basic tax structure he inherits. Nevertheless, the costs associated with this program for Growth with Fairness dictate that some adjustments in federal taxation be made immediately. This program therefore includes four specific tax changes: a new levy on luxury consumption, a new levy on speculative investment, restored progressivity in the individual income tax, and revised tax rules concerning estates. These changes would generate the money necessary to ensure strict fiscal balance. Moreover, they have been consciously designed to raise that money in ways that help to foster growth and advance fairness. Each, therefore, has a substantive as well as a financial justification.

An excise tax on luxury consumption. The first response to a government's need for revenues, given that the existing structure must largely be taken as fixed, is to find something new to tax. The most common proposal of this sort, especially among conservatives, is to impose a levy on personal consumption. Consumption taxes, in the form of excises on specifically listed items, contributed approximately a third of all federal receipts during the 1930s but comprise less than 5 percent today. Most European countries have adopted a sophisticated version of the general sales tax—a value-added tax, based on additions to unit cost at each stage in production. Its potential for generating receipts is enormous. In the United States, however, general sales taxes have traditionally been the domain of the states, which would resent federal intrusion and find themselves the losers in the competition for revenues. Moreover, taxes on personal consumption are inflationary and clearly regressive. To the extent that low-income taxpayers must devote a greater proportion of their earnings to the consumption of necessities than do high-income taxpayers, such taxes burden the poor far more than they do the rich. Experience in Europe shows that this regressive tendency can, in part, be mitigated through a series of exemptions, rebates, and multiple rates. Abandoning uniformity, however, means that the tax is much more complicated to administer and enforce, and it then can become prey to politically motivated manipulations. While a broad national sales tax is extremely objectionable, a more limited tax of this sort can provide revenues and avoid distributional dangers. Specifically, this program calls for a sales tax applicable only to durable and nondurable goods and to personal services priced at $250 or above.

The average household would pay this tax only periodically. It does not purchase a major appliance or gold jewelry or a recreational vehicle every year. The well-to-do house-hold, by contrast, with money to spend on expensive luxu-ries, would find that its tax obligations will increase. The $250 threshold is high enough to exclude most of the necessities of daily living without the political difficulty of having to list particular excluded items. It thus maintains simplicity of administration while avoiding the pitfall of inequity. More than $2.8 trillion a year is spent by Americans on personal consumption, most of it for goods and services priced under the proposed minimum threshold of $250. A flat 4 percent tax on big-ticket items would generate about $15 billion an-nually in new federal revenues, based on recent consumer expenditure surveys. Even better, it is possible to secure the same total revenue through a more discriminating system that imposes lower excise rates on ordinary consumer durables and higher excise rates on special luxuries.

The operative principle should be that those with the greatest capacity to pay, as evidenced by their ability to de-vote more than average sums to high-priced goods, should contribute somewhat more to reduce the economically bur-densome government deficit and to finance programs needed to restore American productivity. Further, because the cost of luxury items would then be somewhat higher, there would be greater incentive for upper-income households to chan-nel more of their discretionary income into savings and in-vestment rather than into personal consumption. Again the result would be positive for American economic competi-tiveness. The introduction of a limited tax on luxuries cost-ing more than $250 would supply needed revenues, would be progressive in that it would affect primarily the relatively wealthy, and would provide market incentives consistent with our program for Growth with Fairness.

A stamp duty on the transfer of securities. The second proposed tax is a 1 percent levy on the sale or purchase of any security (stock, bond, option) that is not newly issued by a corporation or firm. The federal government maintained a stock-transfer tax from 1919 through 1965. Japan, Germany, and the United Kingdom impose fees for the right to trade in their stock markets. Following the suggestion of House Speaker Jim Wright, this program would revive the stock-transfer tax, although in a modified form that exempts original issues. In 1986, U.S. financial markets traded more than $2 trillion worth of securities. Of that total, less than $225 billion was for new issues. At 1 percent of the remainder, a securities transfer tax would generate approximately $35 billion in new revenues, and it would be strongly progressive in its distributional effect. According to a recent study of household wealth commissioned by the Joint Economic Committee of Congress, the top one-tenth of all families own 89 percent of all common stock and 90 percent of all bonds. The vast majority of households, who possess little or no marketable wealth, would be untouched by the tax.

The tax also has an economic usefulness in helping to channel savings into productive plants and equipment. By taxing the transfer of securities that are not newly issued, we could discourage the speculative investment of wealth and encourage investment in the real assets of enterprises. One of the central problems limiting the potential for economic revitalization in the United States is the low level of business outlays for plants and equipment. In 1986, less that 8 percent of GNP was invested in the productive expansion and modernization of our economic base, compared with more than 16 percent in Japan. We must consciously readjust incentives to stimulate the redevelopment of our industrial infrastructure. A good part of the difficulty stems from the fact that the allocation of U.S. savings, already low by comparative standards, has been skewed by the attractiveness of short-run financial returns. Not enough of our savings are being devoted to tangible capital. During the stock market boom of the last few years, the percentage of sales from primary offerings fell by more than half. New issues increase the ability of firms to construct or repair needed physical assets. The secondary manipulation of financial paper, by contrast, is a lucrative but unproductive activity that adds no flow of resources to American manufacturers. The gains of the recent securities bull market mostly passed from investor to investor, rather than from investor to goods-producing firms. In slightly raising the marginal tax cost for speculative behavior, we can help induce those with disposable income to shift the apportionment of their savings. The aim is to structure U.S. tax incentives to make more funds available for the expansion and modernization of our industrial capacity.

Restoring income tax progressivity. In 1960, at the end of the Eisenhower administration, the marginal tax rate in the top federal income tax bracket was 91 percent. By 1988, at the end of the Reagan administration—if there are no further changes in the law—the top marginal rate will be only 28 percent. America is not the only country to have slashed tax rates in recent years, but it has taken this trend to the greatest extreme. Individuals in the richest tax bracket now face a lower marginal tax rate in the United States than in any other OECD nation. The top bracket rate in Japan is 76.5 percent; in Germany it is 56 percent; and even in Britain under Prime Minister Margaret Thatcher it is 60 percent. The Reagan years were a bonanza for the wealthy. Progressivity in the income tax was significantly eroded, sacrificed by the failed policy of supply-side economics. The overall American tax structure, which was barely proportional across income strata during the 1970s, now tilts in a pro-rich direction. The federal revenue code, once committed to the principle of ability to pay, now speaks in a decidedly upper-class accent.

Tax legislation often emerges out of compromise, and the outcome often does not make sense. The 1986 law established only two tax brackets, 15 percent for the first $29,750 of taxable income and 28 percent for all taxable income above that amount. The tax reform package also included an intermediate, five-bracket graduated system for the 1987 transition year. The main difference is a 35 percent marginal rate between $45,000 and $90,000 of taxable income, and a 38.5 percent marginal rate above $90,000. The movement from the transition year rate structure to that of the final bill will cost the federal government approximately $25 billion annually in lost revenues, all of which will flow into the pockets of upper-income taxpayers.

This step would be nullified in this program for Growth with Fairness, which would retain for 1988 and beyond the "transitional" rates presently intended solely for 1987. The resulting tax structure would be much more progressive. It also would be closer to the proposal originally made by President Reagan and to the legislation passed by the Democrats in the House of Representatives. There is no reason, when the government urgently needs revenues to reduce the deficit and to rebuild American industry, that we should proceed to lower the tax rates on the most affluent of our citizens. The economic experiences of the 1980s have shown that lower taxes for those with discretionary incomes do not automatically increase the stock of U.S. savings. There is neither distributional equity nor productive trickle-down in the scheduled final stage of the 1986 tax rate revision. Recouping approximately $25 billion in tax receipts by freezing the status quo is a fair and efficient way to raise the revenues needed to restore our national economic competitiveness.

Taxing the wealth of estates. Despite the American attachment to equal opportunity for all, historically we have been reluctant to tax the wealth amassed by rich individuals before it is passed on to their heirs. Since the end of World War II, the estate tax has never contributed more than 2.6 percent of federal revenues. Moreover, the rates have declined significantly over the past 10 years, especially as part of President Reagan's regressive policies. The present law, once fully phased in, will totally exempt from taxation all estates worth less than $600,000 dollars and will establish graduated rates stretching from 18 to 50 percent on the remainder. Estate taxation will thus raise less than 1 percent of federal receipts and will apply only to the smallest minority of wealthiest estates. In addition, the federal revenue code contains a loophole that allows inherited estates to escape paying their share of the capital gains tax. Although the tax on capital gains is imposed generally on increases in the value of an asset when it is sold or exchanged, it is not now imposed when the transfer results from the death of the holder of the asset. Moreover, even though the tax is not paid in this circumstance, an heir

Budget Changes for Growth with Fairness (by billions of dollars)				
Additional Expenditures			**Additional Revenues and Savings**	
Industrial Develop-			Military weapons	$ 15
ment Bank	$ 10		Agricultural subsidies	$ 10
Public works	$ 25			
Physical resources		$ 35	Luxury consumption tax	$ 15
Federalization	$ 27		Speculative gains tax	$ 35
Welfare reform	$ 8		Income tax progressivity	$ 25
Human resources		$ 35	Taxing wealthy estates	$ 5
Deficit Reduction		$ 35		
TOTAL		$105	TOTAL	$105

is allowed to disregard all appreciation in the value of the asset prior to the time when he or she assumes control of it. Therefore, the gains to the estate realized prior to its transfer to an heir escape untaxed. The result is an enormous benefit to the very wealthy.

As recommended by the Citizens for Tax Justice, the Growth with Fairness program proposes that Congress rescind the latest reductions in the federal estate tax, freezing the top estate tax rate at 50 percent, and that it repeal the loophole allowing built-up capital gains to be totally disregarded at death. These two changes in the treatment of inherited wealth will raise approximately $5 billion annually. The revenues will be derived overwhelmingly from the economic elite of our society. Moreover, these changes in the tax code will encourage a greater turnover of funds in capital markets by removing artificial tax incentives to hold on to portfolio assets in contemplation of death. Increased taxation of the transfer of wealthy estates will also signal a revived emphasis on individual opportunity and productive effort, symbolic of an active and energetic approach to American economic growth. Thus, like the previous tax proposals offered here, these changes in our treatment of estates combine the capacity to generate needed revenues with improved progressivity and appropriate economic incentives. It is this combination of virtues that make them suitable for a program dedicated to Growth with Fairness.

Conclusion

A budget is the codification of the priorities inherent in a political program. Because of the reckless policies of the Reagan administration, federal finances have been thrown into chaos. For the past few years, the federal budget has spoken in negative terms, telling us that we must make do with less. It has become a document reflecting our failures in financial accounts and national productivity.

This must be rectified, both to lower the penalty upon future generations and to remove the burdens that artificially high interest rates place upon domestic investment and international competitiveness. In addition, budget priorities must be adjusted so as to better promote economic growth and social justice. The tax proposals outlined above would generate $80 billion annually in new federal revenues. The spending reforms would save the federal government $25 billion more. This sum would be sufficient to finance the physical capital and the human resources programs for Growth with Fairness and to provide a suitable amount for needed deficit reduction. Proposed here is an activist budget that is prepared to expend money for those services essential to American economic reinvigoration and to raise money in ways that advance tax progressivity and supply useful market incentives.

Chapter 6:

REBUILDING THE AMERICAN ECONOMY

We are entering a new era in which technological innovations are revolutionizing the way goods are produced and services provided. It is an era of global interdependence and expanding opportunities for peace and prosperity. It is also an era of high risk and uncertainty, for it is not guaranteed that America will be able to maintain a preeminent economic position among nations or preserve the affluence to which our citizens have become accustomed. This is the challenge confronting the next generation of American leaders. They must help us adapt to evolving economic conditions while remaining faithful to our American traditions. By the way they articulate our national goals and by the specific policies they propose, our new leaders must arouse us from our complacency and set us firmly on the road to economic renewal. The president elected in 1988 will be responsible for providing this country with that leadership and with a fresh program of action. This is an opportunity that must not be squandered.

Several times in our past the American people have been confronted with fundamental changes in the economy, the society, and the world. In overcoming each of these challenges we have been inspired by a vision of America's expanding future that has animated us since the founding of our republic. Believing that "all men are created equal," we have also believed that all Americans are equally entitled to share in the responsibilities and the benefits of common citizenship. We the people have been guided by the confidence that together we can shape a better future. When possible, we have pursued that destiny through our individual efforts. When necessary, we have called upon our government to fulfill the promise of promoting the general welfare. The ideal of growth with fairness is deeply rooted in our national experience.

Four principles are inherent in that ideal. Neglected over the past few years, they deserve special emphasis: a responsible and supportive government; the necessity of a dynamic, productive, and competitive private sector; a commitment to social fairness for all Americans; and a patriotic pride that is positive and unifying in outlook. These principles have served as a guide in formulating both the critique of existing U.S. policies and the program prescriptions for the decades ahead presented in this book. They are the principles by which Americans must evaluate our government's actions and our economy's performance for the balance of this century.

No objective observer can scrutinize the performance of our national economy today without grave concern for its future. The hard and painful underlying reality is that large segments of our vital manufacturing industries have lost their ability to compete in foreign trade and even in domestic markets. Large numbers of firms have ceased to operate at all within our borders except to import and assemble products now made elsewhere. The effects on our working people and on their communities in many cases have been devastating. Common sense informs us that we cannot continue much longer to run up annual strings of $200 billion budget deficits or $160 billion trade deficits. No society can continue indefinitely to consume far more than it produces, to live year after year far beyond its means, or to prosper primarily by exchanging financial services and by selling hamburgers.

Every year that passes we become more vulnerable to the decisions of foreign investors and bankers. Either they will withdraw their funds or they will keep them in the United States provided that we continue to pay interest rates well above those available elsewhere. With such high interest rates, we will stifle our own firms that need to raise money to modernize their facilities so that they can survive in international markets. Every year that we fail to take effective action we sink deeper into debt. We further weaken our competitiveness and risk the prospect of a long-lasting decline that will progressively undermine our faith in the historic American dream and irreversibly diminish our role in the world economy. Unfortunately, the Reagan administration operated with no strategy whatsoever for averting this impending crisis. When it even admitted a problem, it hoped to make us believe that the metaphysics of the marketplace would miraculously rescue us from the brink.

The objective observer cannot help but notice the stagnation of real family incomes during the past 15 years and the growing disparities in income distribution. Recent tax and fiscal policies sponsored by President Reagan have bloated measurably the purchasing power of the top 20 percent, while budget cuts and an unbalanced economy have savaged the already depressed incomes of the working poor and near poor. The average middle-class family has barely held on to its standard of living, and in the process, it has contracted enormous consumer debt that has reduced our national savings rate to the lowest among the major industrial nations. We should not stand by and do nothing while one out of every five American children lives in poverty each year. We should not stand by when the opportunities available to today's young families are significantly weaker than those that existed for their parents.

Compelling evidence shows that the so-called Reagan recovery of the past few years has been superficial and uneven, and has barely made up for the depths of the previous Reagan recession. More importantly, that recovery has been built upon sand. The Reagan policies weakened rather than strengthened the structural foundations from which sound economic regeneration must proceed. The solution to domestic stagnation and to the loss of international competitiveness is to strengthen industrial productivity. The issue is how this productivity can best be revived, consistent with the American traditions of limited government and inclusive social fairness.

As the American people confront the challenges of the coming decades, we will have to choose among three very different policy directions. We can continue to drift in the sea of free market economics, hoping that some self-correcting processes of marginal adjustment will automatically save us from future decline. This option, which remains the fixed ideology of the Reagan administration and will probably characterize the policies of any likely Republican successor, is based entirely on wishful thinking. An economy once undermined cannot easily propel itself back into efficient operation. The second alternative focuses correctly on the twin towers of our current deficits—budgetary and international—as sources of economic strain that can only be reversed by determined public policy. Yet the proposed solution is to attack these deficits simply by means of severe retrenchment, using a combination of deep cutbacks in federal expenditures, mostly on the domestic side, and arbitrary protectionism against imports, mostly to retaliate against our main trade competitors. If rigorously applied, these measures would squeeze down the deficits, but at a devastating cost to our living standards and those of the rest of the world. Such draconian measures are neither necessary nor desirable. The American people need not impose such suffering on themselves or on others. Moreover, any embrace of such measures by the Democratic party would violate its historic reputation as the party of growth and fairness and would lead to electoral disaster.

The third option, the one advocated in this book, calls for energetic and coordinated efforts to rebuild our industrial productivity and to distribute its benefits equitably. It is not enough have faith in the capacities of our private sector or to seek to reverse the consequences of misguided Reagan priorities. We must initiate positive measures that use the legitimate influence of government to enable us once again to regain control of our national economic future. Those measures would be targeted efficiently and would require vigorous leadership by the federal government and close cooperation with state and local authorities, investors, managers, workers, and community associations. They would be based on a sound understanding of the importance of the tasks that lie ahead and would reflect a national commitment to solve them pragmatically and decisively.

The standard for a proper U.S. government policy were set forth by Alexander Hamilton as early as 1774:

> To render it agreeable to good policy, three things are requisite. First, that the necessity of the times requires it; second, that it not be the probable source of greater evils than those it pretends to remedy; and lastly, that it have a probability of success.

This program for Growth with Fairness has been guided by Hamilton's standards. The times do require strong and effective action, while to continue with free market drift or to reply merely with negative retrenchment will cost America much of her prosperity at home and much of her leading position in the world economy. These proposals will place new demands upon the capacity of our government and new expectations upon our citizens, but the potential intrinsic to our democracy is enormous, and the evils that must be eradicated attack the historic foundations of our way of life. Public policy cannot hope and should not try to remedy social evils by itself, but the proposals advanced here have a high probability of success, assured by the previous experiences of our own government and by successful programs implemented by governments in other countries.

Some policy proposals outlined in this book will require legislation by Congress; others can be implemented by executive authority. Some already exist on the national agenda; others are more innovative and novel. The book does not offer a complete list of all feasible reforms; there are other ideas that could have been included. The goal was to present a coherent vision for the American economic future and to emphasize policies that best fulfill that vision. These recommendations form the essential core of a practical, effective, and responsible program to restore America's tradition of growth with fairness.

To recapitulate the main proposals, this program for Growth with Fairness calls for

- The establishment of a federal Industrial Development Bank, which would provide equity capital for the expansion and modernization of industries that will create jobs and promote our technological leadership in world markets, or that are necessary for national defense or economic security. The Bank would cooperate with state-level development institutions and private lenders, and its funds would be made available only to those firms that formally commit themselves to approved modernization plans.

- A substantial program of infrastructure investment to rehabilitate our deteriorating national stock of roads, bridges, and sewage treatment and mass transit facilities. Such public goods are a necessary prerequisite for private productive growth.

- A vigorous trade policy intended to improve our long-term competitive potential. It would ensure against product dumping in American markets, prevent discrimination against U.S. products in foreign markets, and enact "modernization tariffs" that would guarantee, for a specified and limited time, preferential access to domestic markets to those industries that commit themselves to approved modernization plans.

- A new federal compact with the states, by which the central government would assume responsibility for welfare and Medicaid costs and ensure minimum acceptable program standards. In exchange, the states would apply their savings to promoting economic development and to improving and expanding education, job training, day care, and other human services. Such efforts would simultaneously reduce dependency and contribute to economic growth and job creation.

- Adjusted budgetary priorities needed to implement these programs and provide a more responsible fiscal policy. The fiscal plan proposes to devote $35 billion in additional funds to deficit reduction, and the same amount to physical infrastructure/industrial development and to human resources/welfare reform. The $105 billion in additional revenues would be derived, first, by shifting expenditures away from excessive acquisitions of military hardware and from subsidies to corporate agribusiness, and, second, by garnering greater tax revenues. This fiscal plan would restore progressivity to the top bracket of the personal income tax, raise additional revenues from the estates of the wealthy, levy an excise on luxury consumption, and impose a new tax on all transactions in speculative securities.

In advocating the simultaneous pursuit of growth and fairness, this book explicitly rejects the dismal notion that these are incompatible goals, that more of one means less of the other. The Kennedy and Johnson years, which witnessed unprecedented and sustained growth in our national economy, was also the era of greatest progress toward social fairness.

The rejection of fairness as a goal of social policy during the Reagan period has contributed nothing to economic growth. Growth and fairness are mutually reinforcing. More of one can and should mean more of the other. This has been the substance of the American dream, and it is as valid today as it has been throughout our history.

Our economic future is clouded by uncertainty. It depends partly on international forces beyond our direct control, partly on technical grounds that no one can predict. There is much, however, that we as a people can do to chart the economic and social future we desire, and many instruments are available to us through government and the other institutions of our society to make that future a living reality. Economic life is not governed entirely by mysterious, impersonal, or occult forces beyond the reach of human intelligence and will, to which we must fatalistically adapt. Economic institutions, including economic markets, are man-made structures whose performance depends on the way we treat them. Japan's economic successes in recent years have been the result of human determination reinforced by sound and vigorous government policy. Our stagnation can be traced in large measure to confusion over economic goals and to wrongheaded, perverse, and mean-spirited government policies.

These failures of policy in recent years can be corrected. As a people we have never been prepared to wait passively for good things to happen—to depend, for example, on promises of automatic adjustments or economic miracles to save us from the consequences of misplaced priorities or incompetent economic management. We have always been a forward-looking, robust, and active people. When we recognize common problems we mobilize our resources and take positive action to deal with them. In short, we have always believed we can take charge of our shared destiny.

We have in abundance all the natural, physical, and human resources needed to realize the optimistic vision of our common future outlined in the first chapter of this volume. This is the future of increasing material abundance, fairly distributed, that has animated Americans since the founding of our society. We have always expected that individuals, families, communities, and enterprises would do all they could to secure their livelihoods on their own. We have also considered our government to be an active partner, doing through our democratic institutions what we could not accomplish for ourselves as individuals. Restoring government to its proper and active role is essential today to the rejuvenation of our national economy.

During this century the American people have looked to the Democratic party for leadership when their future seemed to be blocked. The Democratic party has been willing to adopt bold and decisive measures when caution and conventional approaches have failed. Democrats have always been sensitive and responsive to the needs and aspirations of the majority of our people. They have been inclined to use the resources of our democratic government to achieve our national purposes. Like FDR during the Republican depression of the 1930s, they have known how to convert fear into hope, paralysis into accomplishment. This is precisely what the American people expect.

The economic disquiet that looms over our lives today is a challenge to the statesmanship of the Democratic party. Either it will seize the opportunity—through positive measures such as those proposed in this program—to reverse the dangerous drift and decline in our national economy, the polarization of our society, and the needless human costs that are the consequence of the Reagan administration's abdication of responsibility, or it will betray by meek and expedient compromises its historic role in American politics. The challenge is here; the means are at hand.

REFERENCES

DATA SOURCES

Children's Defense Fund. *A Children's Defense Budget.* FY 1987.

Council of Economic Advisers. *Economic Report of the President.* 1987.

Economist. World Business Cycles. The Economist Newspaper Ltd., London, 1982.

International Labor Organization. *Yearbook of Labor Statistics.* 1986.

Mellor, Earl F. "Workers at the Minimum Wage or Less," *Monthly Labor Review* (July 1987): 34–38.

Organization for Economic Cooperation and Development. *Economic Outlook.*

Organization for Economic Cooperation and Development. *Observer.*

Organization for Economic Cooperation and Development. *Revenue Statistics of OECD Member Countries.*

Securities and Exchange Commission. *Monthly Statistical Review.*

Tax Foundation, Inc. *Facts and Figures on Government Finance.* 1986.

The Conference Board. *Manufacturing Investment Statistics.*

U.S. Bureau of the Census. *Current Population Reports.* Series P-60, no. 157. "Money Income and Poverty Status of Families and Persons in the United States." 1986.

U.S. Department of Commerce, International Trade Administration. *U.S. Industrial Outlook.*

U.S. Department of Commerce. *Statistical Abstract of the United States.* 1987.

U.S. Department of Commerce. *Survey of Current Business.*

U.S. Department of Health and Human Services. *Characteristics of State Plans for Aid to Families with Dependent Children.* 1987.

U.S. Department of Health and Human Services, Health Care Financing Administration. *The Medicare and Medicaid Data Book.* 1983.

U.S. Department of Health and Human Services. *Social Security Bulletin, Annual Statistical Supplement.* 1987.

U.S. Office of Management and Budget. *The Budget of the United States Government.* FY 1988.

U.S. Office of Management and Budget. *The Budget of the United States, Historical Tables.* FY 1988.

---

* Several data sources that were consulted are issued periodically, whether monthly, quarterly, or annually. Where no specific date of publication is listed after a source, several issues of that serial were used. Specific references to these sources accompany the figures and tables in the body of this book.

REFERENCE SOURCES

Anderson, Gerald H., and John B. Carlson. "Does Dollar Depreciation Matter: the Case of Auto Imports from Japan." *Economic Commentary* (Federal Reserve Bank of Cleveland), 1 May, 1987.

Associated General Contractors of America. *America's Infrastructure: A Plan to Rebuild.* Washington, D.C., May 1983.

Bergsten, C. Fred. "Gearing up for World Growth," *Challenge* (May-June 1986): 35–40.

Bluestone, Barry and Bennett Harrison. *The Deindustrialization of America.* New York: Basic Books, 1982.

Citizens for Tax Justice. *The Failure of Corporate Tax Incentives.* Washington, D.C.: Citizens for Tax Justice, 1985.

Citizens for Tax Justice. *Meeting the Revenue Targets in the 1988 Budget.* Washington, D.C.: Citizens for Tax Justice, May 1987.

Choate, Pat, and Susan Walter. *America in Ruins.* Washington, D.C.: Council of State Planning Agencies, 1981.

Cockburn, Alexander, and Robert Pollin. "How to Talk About Economic Strategy." *The Nation,* 28 February, 1987, 245–247.

Congressional Budget Office. *The Industrial Policy Debate.* Washington, D.C.: U.S. GPO, 1983.

Congressional Budget Office. *The Federal Budget for Public Works Infrastructure.* Washington, D.C.: U.S. GPO, 1985.

Congressional Budget Office. *The Federal Role in State Industrial Development Programs.* Washington, D.C.: U.S. GPO, 1984.

Congressional Budget Office. *Medicaid: Choices for 1982 and Beyond.* Washington, D.C.: U.S. GPO, 1981.

Corcoran, Mary, Greg J. Duncan, Gerald Gurin, and Patricia Gurin, "Myth and Reality: The Causes and Persistence of Poverty," *Journal of Policy Analysis and Management* (Summer 1985): 516–537.

Daggett, Stephen and Jo L. Husbands. *Achieving an Affordable Defense.* Washington, D.C.: The Committee for National Security, 1987.

Data Resources Inc. (DRI) and Associated General Contractors of America. *America's Infrastructure: Study of a $10 Billion Annual Infrastructure Investment.* Washington, D.C., October 1984.

Danziger, Sheldon, and Peter Gottschalk. "Families with Children Have Fared Worst." *Challenge* (March-April 1986): 40–47.

Danziger, Sheldon, and Peter Gottschalk. "Target Support at Children and Families." *New York Times, 22 March, 1987.*

DeGrasse, Robert, Jr., with Paul Murphy and William Ragen. The Costs and Consequences of Reagan's Military Buildup. New York: Council on Economic Priorities, 1982.

Epstein, Joshua M. *The 1988 Defense Budget.* Washington, D.C.: Brookings Institution, 1987.

Gordon, David L. *Development Finance Companies, State and Privately Owned.* Washington, D.C.: World Bank, 1983.

Kaufmann, William W. *A Reasonable Defense Budget* Washington, D.C.: Brookings Institution, 1986.

Krasner, Stephen D. "United States Commercial and Monetary Policy: Unravelling the Paradox of External Strength and Internal Weakness." In *Between Power and Plenty,* ed. Peter J. Katzenstein. Madison: University of Wisconsin Press, 1978.

Ledebur, Larry, David Rasmussen, and Bill Hamilton. *Economic Development in the Post-Federal Era: Innovations in State Industrial Development.* Washington, D.C.: The Urban Institute, June 1984.

Levitan, Sar. *Programs in Aid of the Poor.* 5th ed. Baltimore, Md.: Johns Hopkins Press, 1985.

Levy, Michael S., and Richard C. Michel. "An Economic Bust for the Baby Boom." *Challenge* (March-April 1986): 33–39.

Organization for Economic Cooperation and Development. "The Origins of High Real Interest Rates." *OECD Economic Studies #5* (Autumn 1985): 7–57.

Palmer, John L., and Isabel V. Sawhill, eds. *The Reagan Experiment.* Washington, D.C.: Brookings Institution, 1982.

Palmer, John L., and Isabel V. Sawhill, eds. *The Reagan Record.* Washington, D.C.: Brookings Institution, 1984.

Pechman, Joseph A. *Federal Tax Policy,* 5th ed. Washington, D.C.: Brookings Institution, 1987.

Pechman, Joseph A. *Who Paid the Taxes, 1966–85?* Washington, D.C.: Brookings Institution, 1985.

Pempel, T.J. "Japanese Foreign Economic Policy: The Domestic Basis for International Behavior." In *Between Power and Plenty,* ed. Peter J. Katzenstein. Madison: University of Wisconsin Press, 1978.

Reinshuttle, Robert J. *Economic Development: A Survey of State Activities.* Lexington, Ky.: Council of State Governments, 1983.

U.S. Congress, Joint Economic Committee. *Hard Choices.* Washington, D.C.: U.S. GPO, 1984.

U.S. Congress, Joint Economic Committee. *Impact of the 1981 Personal Income Tax Reductions on Income Distribution.* Washington, D.C.: U.S. GPO, 1982.

U.S. International Trade Commission. *Annual Report.* Washington, D.C.: U.S. GPO.

Viner, Jacob. *International Economics.* Glencoe,Ill.: Free Press, 1951.

Weinberg, Daniel H. "Poverty Spending and the Poverty Gap." *Journal of Policy Analysis and Management* (Winter 1987): 230-241.

Welter, Therese R. "Hurdling: U.S. Companies are Sharing Some of the Risks and Costs." *Industry Week*, 13 July, 1987.

Whicker, Marcia Lynn, and Raymond A. Moore. "Policies to Build a More Competitive America." Paper prepared for presentation at the 1987 American Political Science Association meetings, Chicago, Ill., 1987.

Whyte, William Foote. "Economic Folklore and Corporate Takeovers: Position Paper Submitted to Democratic Policy Commission." 1987.

Zysman, John and Stephen Cohen. *Manufacturing Matters: The Myth of the Post-Industrial Economy.* New York: Basic Books, 1987.

About the Authors:

Milton J. Esman, Steven I. Jackson, and Ronald F. King are members of the Department of Government at Cornell University. Esman's specific field of expertise is comparative politics and public administration, Jackson's is international political economy, and King's is domestic public finance.